THE
SUBMARINE
BOOK

CHUCK LAWLISS

BURFORD BOOKS

Printed in the United States of America.

10 9 8 7 6 5 4 3 2 1

Library of Congress Cataloging-in-Publication Data
Lawliss, Chuck
     The submarine book: an illustrated history of the attack
     submarine / by Chuck Lawliss
            p.   cm.
     Originally published: New York: Thames and Hudson, 1991.
     Includes bibliographical references.
     ISBN 1-58080-078-5 (pb)
     1. Nuclear submarines—United States. I. Title.
V857.5.L39   2000
359.9'383—dc21   00-040331

Contents

1 | We Know We're Ready to Attack

During the Cold War, in secret places deep in the oceans of the world, down where the last traces of light vanish, huge U.S. Navy ballistic submarines would lie still in the water "on station," their nuclear missiles locked on key targets in the former Soviet Union. Smaller fast-attack submarines, also nuclear powered, were on constant patrol, often within a few miles of the Russian coast, seeking hostile submarines and monitoring their activities. Russian submarines, ballistic and fast attack, were busy doing the same. Submarine fleets behaved like rival street gangs, armed to the teeth, each protecting its turf while probing for a weakness in the enemy. Today ballistic submarines are still on station and fast-attack submarines still patrol the deep, but these are training exercises, designed to keep submariners and their weapons in top shape.

A modern U.S. attack submarine, the USS Seawolf, *on sea trials.*

The mobility, secrecy, and sheer firepower of a ballistic submarine make it the most lethal weapon ever devised by man. The warheads on one ballistic-missile submarine can destroy a dozen cities. If all the presently deployed ballistic submarines fired their missiles, the world as we know it would end within the hour.

Little is known about nuclear submarines outside the military. A submarine is secretive by design. The submarine command of the U.S. Navy has been called the "Silent Service," and the epithet is well deserved.

Little is known about the men who run the nuclear submarines, either. Much of what they do and what they experience at sea is secret, even from their families and friends. They are all males, all volunteers, above average in intelligence, better educated than most servicemen, and have a flair for mechanics or electronics. Many were computer literate before joining the Navy. They receive extra pay for serving aboard submarines, and they earn it.

A nuclear submarine can stay submerged for months, a long time to go without sunlight, fresh air, time off. It's a long time to go without family, girls, sports, sex, a cold beer. Life aboard a nuclear submarine is a continuous round of work, drills, sleep, and a minimum of quiet recreation in spaces that are claustrophobic at best. From the captain on down, everyone has enormous responsibilities, to one another, to the submarine and its nuclear power plant, to the missiles, to national defense. And danger lurks even in peacetime. Submarines, like airplanes, do not tolerate mistakes.

The nuclear submarine is a relatively new weapon, its resemblance to earlier submarines mostly superficial. Until many years after World War II, the submarine wasn't even a true submarine, a vessel whose natural habitat is under-

The attack submarine USS Pogy surfaces through an Arctic ice floe at sunrise.

water. It was a diesel-powered vessel that could submerge and operate underwater for a limited time on battery power. When the batteries ran down, or the air gave out, it had to surface. Those are the characteristics of a submersible, not a submarine. The old submarines were armed with torpedoes, imperfect weapons at best. Despite these limitations, Hitler's submarines nearly drove Britain out of the war, and U.S. submarines were instrumental in the defeat of Japan.

In 1962 the first true submarine was launched, the nuclear-powered *Nautilus,* appropriately named after Jules Verne's fictional submarine. The *Nautilus* could do things that an earlier generation would have scorned as fantasy—travel underwater for months at a time, often at speeds in excess of thirty knots, sail around the world submerged, pass under the polar ice cap.

The next major development was inevitable: arming the nuclear-powered submarine with nuclear weapons. The first submarine missiles were crude, short range, unguid-

ed, and inaccurate. But each generation of submarine-fired missiles was a giant step forward. Polaris, Poseidon, Tridents I and II progressively increased in range, explosive power, accuracy, and the ability to evade enemy detection while in flight.

An officer searches for surface ships with a periscope aboard the Los Angeles–class fast-attack submarine USS Tucson.

These improvements brought about a change in the nuclear submarine's role in defense strategy. Conventional military wisdom once envisioned the following scenario for a nuclear war: the Soviet Union launches its missiles first; the United States discovers the launch before the Soviet missiles strike and launches a retaliatory attack; both nations are nearly destroyed, neither is the winner. This bleak prospect was considered to be the ultimate deterrent to nuclear warfare.

At first, the U.S. retaliatory strike capacity consisted of intercontinental ballistic-missile (ICBM) silos and Strategic Air Command (SAC) planes carrying nuclear bombs. Nuclear submarines were added to the mix when their missiles became capable of reaching Russian targets with an adequate payload from an acceptable distance with reasonable accuracy.

Ballistic submarines outgrew this supplementary role when they achieved the ability to hit and destroy targets from nearly 2,000 miles away. Because ballistic submarines operate close to shore, their missiles can reach enemy targets such as missile silos before missiles launched from SAC bombers or a silo. This is vital; seconds will be the margin of victory in a nuclear war. If nuclear war comes, the first shot probably will be fired by a ballistic-missile submarine.

These huge SSBNs, "boomers" in Navy slang, are guarded by fast-attack submarines while the SSBNs are on station. Fast-attack submariners refer to the SSBNs as "hotels." A torpedoman explains, "They're big enough to be a hotel, and they just go out and park there for a couple of months."

Fast-attack submarines are capable of diving to 1,475 feet and traveling submerged at speeds "in excess of thirty knots"—*well* in excess of thirty knots, according to military experts. They patrol right up to foreign coasts and, when hostile submarines emerge, stick with them wherever in the

A Tomahawk missile is secured on board a Los Angeles–class submarine.

world they may go. If a warship or plane went as close to foreign naval bases, it would create an international incident.

Killers as well as hunters, fast-attack submarines are armed with strategic cruise missiles with ranges of up to 1,500 miles. They also carry torpedoes, the traditional submarine weapon. Their Mark 48 torpedoes have a range of more than six miles and use on-board sonar to home in on a target. If the torpedoes miss, they attack again and again. Fast-attack submarines can attack other submarines, surface ships, and land targets.

The crew of a fast-attack submarine numbers fourteen officers and 128 enlisted men, all superbly trained. It takes as long to earn the dolphins of a submariner as it does the

A crewmember on the attack submarine USS Norfolk *crawls into a torpedo tube for a postlaunch inspection.*

wings of a pilot. After submarine school, an enlisted submariner spends up to a year in school learning to be a sonar-
man, torpedoman, electronics technician, or machinist's mate.

Getting aboard a fast-attack submarine requires dexter-
ity. Missiles, torpedoes, and supplies are lowered through
hatches in the hull directly to their resting places, but
humans climb down a narrow ladder on the side of the
"sail," then down another ladder inside the submarine's
pressure hull. The sail, called the "conning tower" on prenu-
clear submarines, is the equivalent of a ship's flying bridge,
serving as the captain's command post while on the surface.
Rising from the sail are a windshield, two periscopes, and a
variety of antennas, all of which retract when the submarine
submerges. Even cleats are turned upside down, their covers
forming a smooth surface with the hull. An exposed cleat or

A crewman exits from the main hatch of the USS Seawolf,
one of the navy's newest submarines.

an extended antenna creates noise. The biggest advantage of a submarine is not how fast or how deep it can go, but how silently.

On the surface, a submarine tosses and rolls; the hull is designed for running submerged, and no concessions are made for surface running. There is little wake. Wake is turbulence, and turbulence is noise. Submarines leaving and entering their bases are monitored by Russian spy satellites. A submarine's position is assumed to be known to the Russians until after it crosses the edge of the continental shelf and dives deep.

A captain of a fast-attack submarine says, "We pride ourselves on the ability to remain undetected, and the ability to inflict greater harm on someone than we would encounter. Actually, if we ever had to go to war, this is one of the safest platforms you could be on.

"I don't think I could operate in the private sector," he adds. "When I assign somebody to do something, I expect it to be done to the standards we demand. There is no room for error. You can't come back and say, 'We installed the depth charges incorrectly,' or 'Sorry, but we are going out on strike today.' Our safety and the safety of our country depend on us doing the job correctly.

"We know we are ready to attack. There is no doubt in my mind that if we had to go out and operate against an enemy, we'd fulfill our mission."

When it is time to dive, the men in the sail go below. A ladder leads down a narrow vertical pipe to the warm, well-lighted control room. On one side, two young sailors sit facing an array of digital readouts and electronic displays. They work steering wheels resembling those of light planes. One sailor, the helmsman, controls the horizontal course; the other, the planesman, controls the depth. Seated behind

At the controls of the fast-attack sub USS Tucson.

them quietly giving commands is the diving officer. Only the changing numbers on the depth gauge give evidence that the submarine is headed down under tons of cold seawater.

Every needed bit of information is on display some-where in this thirty-by-thirty-foot room, and someone is monitoring each display. To the untrained eye, the scene is too complex to comprehend. To a submariner, it is simply an efficient way to check on the submarine's vital signs.

One instrument seems out of place, so low tech as to be an anachronism. It is the inclinometer, as uncomplicated as the glass part of a carpenter's level, which it resembles. The position of the bubble indicates the submarine's precise angle of incline or decline from horizontal. While diving or rising, the planesman must "keep the bubble" at exactly the degree called for. "I've lost the bubble" means "I'm con-fused and in trouble."

Sensors are needed because no visual information is available in a submerged submarine. The crew is sealed off from the sea. A surface ship heightens the senses; a submarine dulls them. A storm may be raging on the surface, but it doesn't intrude. The sense of movement and isolation is similar to being on a plane cruising at 35,000 feet. Indeed, a submarine behaves like a plane flying underwater.

Just aft of the control room is the sonar room. Bathed in a low green light, six operators sit in front of screens, watching sound as well as listening to it. What looks like luminous green sand drifts down their screens, each grain representing a blip of detected sound. Red and green lights glow on panels linking powerful computers with hydrophones outside the hull. Sonar enables the submarine to grope through the blackness of the depths, alert to anything nearby.

The ocean does strange things to sound waves. Sound travels more than four times as fast in water as it does in the air. Thermoclines, the boundaries between warm and cold layers of water, can reflect sound the way a mirror reflects light. Sometimes sound waves travel through water in straight lines, sometimes in arcs. Sound travels faster in warm water and in water under pressure. It will go down to the ocean floor, bounce up, then go back down again, in a manner similar to radio waves traveling in the air. Because of this property of sound waves, a ship may be detected at certain distances but not at others. Compared to sonar, radar is simple.

Computers are part of the equipment of a modern submarine. Among other functions, they process sonar data and translate it into fire control instructions. Despite the abundance of electronics aboard, U.S. naval policy discourages automation, believing that people make fewer mistakes than do machines, and can correct their mistakes faster. At a depth of 900 feet, a computer controlling the diving planes could malfunction and drive the submarine below crush depth in seconds, causing an implosion that would strew the wreckage for miles on the ocean floor. The Russians, however, have automated many submarine functions, with the objective of smaller crews in smaller submarines.

All equipment is separated from the hull by thick rubber washers and rests on rubber cushions to reduce noise. The nuclear reactor produces steam to turn the turbines, and the turbines whine. The cooling pumps for the reactor, air conditioners, and compressors produce noise. To the degree the noise reaches the hull, it is transmitted into the ocean. Hydrophones on the exterior of the hull monitor the noise from inside the submarine. Accelerometers are used to detect any unnecessary vibration in rotating objects, and noisy parts are replaced immediately. A constant hum can be heard aboard, but careful design keeps it low.

The control room is the one place aboard where you can tell day from night. During daylight hours the overhead fluorescent lights are on. At sunset the room is "rigged for red"; a number of tiny red lights come on, eerily illuminating the controls, accustoming the eye to the dark. Should the submarine surface quickly, the watch officer and others from the control room would go above the instant the sail broke the surface, and they can't spare precious moments adjusting to the dark. Leaving the control room at night, watch personnel wear red goggles to retain night vision.

A third of the crew is nearly always asleep. Berthing areas are lit by dim red lights. The other working areas are lit all the time. Day and night lose their meaning. The passage of time is measured by work, sleep, and meals.

As there is no sense of night and day, there is no sense of the season. The temperature and humidity aboard are

kept at a uniform, comfortable level. And no sense of week-
ends or holidays, since the routine never varies.

Space is at a premium. The aft half of the submarine is
engineering space, housing the reactor and the turbines. In
the bow: missiles, torpedoes, and sonar equipment. Every
nook and cranny has something in it. The cream-colored
bulkheads and passageways are lined with cables and pipes,
and sprinkled with valves and gauges. Sailors must turn side-
ways to pass one another. Taller sailors constantly duck to
avoid banging their heads.

Only the captain has his own cabin, as small as a single
compartment on a train. The bunk folds up to provide him
with a small desk. The other officers live three to an equal-
ly small cabin, their bunks stacked three-up, the lowest at
floor level.

An enlisted man sleeps on a bunk, or "rack," three feet
by six feet with a twenty-six-inch clearance, and it is difficult
for a big man to roll over. On the bunks are camouflage
blankets of a synthetic material. "They don't make lint," an
officer explains. "We used to have wool blankets, but the lint
clogged the air filters." Beneath the bedding under a ply-
wood cover is a four-inch-deep locker where the sailor keeps
his worldly goods. In each bunk space are earphone jacks to
plug into an entertainment system offering several types of
music. A religious channel is popular, perhaps because no
services are held aboard.

A "sailor's bunk is really his kingdom," an officer
explains. "It's the only spot that's really his, his little niche.
When he gets upset and has to get away from it all, he can't
go topside and take a walk on deck."

There are ninety-six bunks for enlisted men, and often
there are more sailors aboard than that. Some bed down in
the torpedo room, some use air mattresses anywhere there's

sufficient floor space. For others it means hot-racking: three men for every two racks, sleeping in shifts.

Submarine duty is tough, and captains try to make things easier for the crew. Uniform regulations are more relaxed than in any other branch of the service. The crew wears blue or black coveralls, called "poopie suits," and running shoes, or "topsiders."

The crew receives no mail while on patrol, but familygrams are relayed by radio. A sailor gives a pad of familygrams to his parents, wife, or girlfriend, and he may receive a short message while at sea. There are no outgoing personal messages of any kind; radio transmissions are too easily detected.

Submarines occasionally will pull into a foreign port and the crew will be given liberty. If that's not on the schedule, the captain may bring the submarine up to periscope depth and let a few sailors look through it briefly, a treat called "periscope liberty."

Relaxation time aboard the USS Hawkbill, *en route to the North Pole.*

The nuclear age brought many improvements to the life of a submariner, but none so welcome as plentiful fresh water. A World War II submariner on patrol might be allowed one or two showers a week; today showers are a daily affair. The shower routine, however, remains the same: get in, turn on the water, get wet, turn off the water, soap up, turn on the water, rinse, turn off the water.

Submariners still grow beards at sea, but they must be shaved off at the end of the patrol. A beard contest usually is held aboard toward the end of the patrol. And some submariners still have the dolphins and conning tower symbol tattooed on their arms.

At the start of a patrol, the crew seems easygoing and congenial, but about two weeks out, edginess begins. Some sailors become irritable and snappish; they calm down and others start in—all as predictable as the tide. Another predictable phenomenon: the crew will get silly the final days at sea. The Navy calls this "channel fever."

No psychiatrist is aboard, nor even a doctor. The physical well-being of the captain and crew is the responsibility of a senior pharmacist mate, trained to operate independently. Medical equipment and supplies are stowed in a space the size of a hall closet. Should someone be critically sick or severely injured, the pharmacist mate may recommend to the captain that the submarine be brought to the surface so that he can consult with a Navy doctor by radio, or that the man be evacuated by helicopter. The final decision rests with the captain.

Like nuclear-powered surface ships, submarines generate power and produce fresh water. But submarines also make their own air. Special generators produce oxygen by electrically hydrolyzing water. The air aboard is monitored constantly for contaminants and the proper mix of gases, oxygen, carbon dioxide, and nitrogen. A complex mechanism continuously "scrubs" the air of carbon dioxide. A byproduct of this process is gaseous hydrogen, which is expelled into the ocean through a diffuser, since big bubbles might be visible on the surface.

No aerosol sprays are allowed on board—no cans of deodorants, shaving cream, lighter fluid, shoe polish, or paint that can adversely affect the ozone level. Yet sailors may smoke aboard, in places and at times designated by the captain.

A fast-attack submarine puts to sea with sufficient food for sixty days. Each day the crew consumes twenty-five loaves of bread, twenty-eight gallons of milk, and ten pounds of coffee. The bread is baked aboard; dough takes less room to store than packaged loaves. Foodstuffs are stored in sequence so that the ingredients for each day's menu are always close at hand. At the beginning of a patrol, the freezer and dry-goods storage areas are full, and the overflow of canned goods spills into the crew's mess. Submariners have to walk over their food until they eat their way through it.

The fresh foods—fruits, vegetables, milk—are gone before the patrol is half over, and the cook switches to food that has been frozen, dehydrated, or canned. If a nuclear submarine didn't run out of food, it could stay submerged indefinitely. Garbage on a submerged submarine goes out the TDU (trash disposal unit), a vertical tube that ejects packaged garbage, weighted to sink to the bottom.

Submarine food is considered the best in the Navy. Meals are served from the stove, not a steam table, and there is table service, not a chow line. There isn't room to do it any other way. "Our cooks are vital to morale," the captain says. "If a sailor has a crummy meal, he's going to be grouchy all day."

Food on submarines is traditionally some of the best in the navy.

Or all night. A meal is served every six hours; the mid-night meal is called "midrats." In addition, a sailor can go in the galley and make a sandwich anytime he wants and help himself to coffee, milk, sodas, a fruit punch called "bug juice," and soft ice cream. Between meals the mess, the only open area on the submarine, serves as a lecture and training area, a study and reading room, an entertainment center, and a place to shoot the breeze. No alcoholic beverages are allowed aboard U.S. submarines.

Officers eat the same food as the enlisted men, but in the tiny officers' mess and with a touch of class. Stewards wear short red jackets and behave as formally as waiters in a fine restaurant. The officers' wardroom also leads a double life as meeting room and recreation area. And should the pharmacist mate have need of an operating table, the ward-room table is at his disposal.

Among the busiest sailors aboard are those fresh from submarine school, still earning their silver dolphins. These "non-quals" are taught firsthand how a submarine operates, a learning process that may take a year. The training is intense. Submariners must know every major system aboard, be able to describe how it works, draw it, and recite its parameters: what alarms are associated with what systems, and where the overrides are for all the hydraulic valves.

It isn't unusual, according to a chief petty officer, for some men to work almost nonstop for twenty-four or thirty hours while underway. "The sacrifices that men make on fast-attack submarines are unbelievable," he says. "They get damn little time off. They average, I would say, sixty to eighty hours a week when we're in port. Last year we were away from our home port 70 percent of the time. We have a schedule, but on a fast attack it's set in quicksand. We've got more things to cover than we've got submarines. We got an emergency call in one day that said we were going out the next morning. We didn't know how long. It was forty-odd days later when we finally pulled in."

Besides the work, the training, and the watches, there are daily drills. The claxon blares. The nature of the "emergency" is announced on the intercom: fire in the reactor room, flooding in the torpedo room, a crash dive. Sleepers roll out of bed and join the men racing to their stations. Submariners learn to go to sleep fast and wake up fast. Every drill is timed. In a real emergency, a few seconds can mean the difference between life and death.

There is little time for recreation and it is mostly electronic. There are movie cassettes, one for each day of the patrol, a personal computer with a selection of video games, a small library. Some sailors bring their hobbies aboard. A torpedoman sketches his shipmates. A machinist's mate builds a sailing ship in a bottle. Traditionalists play cards.

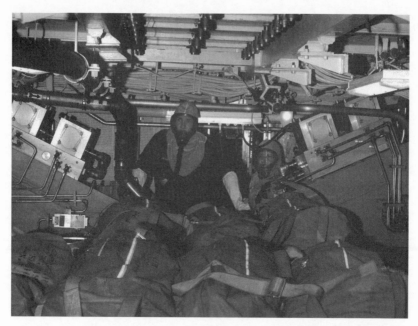

An emergency team trains during a simulated missile fuel leak aboard the new attack submarine USS Seawolf.

Exercise equipment is tucked into nooks and crannies. A rowing machine. Barbells. A stationary bicycle. A workout is an antidote to the enforced immobility of submarine life. There are no sunlamps, however. Submariners are always pale.

Submariners, like all armed services members, must stay in shape and pass semiannual tests comprised of sit-ups, pull-ups, and a timed distance run. They also must keep their weight below proscribed levels. Those failing to meet the minimum standard are put on a training regimen; to fail twice usually means returning to civilian life.

No other part of the armed forces has more top secret equipment or performs more top secret missions. Exciting things happen on patrol that submariners can't talk about. The submarine command discourages publicity, but submariners do speak candidly about some aspects of their lives.

*The crew dons emergency breathing gear during an exercise
on the USS Pogy, beneath the Arctic Circle.*

Submariners are elitists. They see themselves as a cut
above the rest of the Navy. An electronics technician says, "I
never want to go to sea on a skimmer [a submariner's term
for a surface ship]. Hey, there are only two kinds of ships—
submarines and targets."

But even elitists have problems. One married submariner relates, "My daughter, she's three, says, 'Daddy,
don't go to work. Please don't.' And when I come back, for
the first week she won't come to me. It's nerve racking."
Another says, "It's like getting a divorce twice a year." His
friend chimes in, "Hey, I think it's like going on a honey-
moon twice a year." Everyone laughs.

A young radioman complains, "My wife said to me,
'Look, sweetheart, either you're married to me or you're
married to that goddamn sub. Which is it?'"

A major strain on a marriage is that while the man is at sea his wife becomes accustomed to making all the decisions. When he comes home, he takes charge, or attempts to. By the time things have settled down, he's off again.

The divorce rate in the Navy is the highest of all the services, still higher among submariners. Some 20 percent of enlisted submariners leave the service every year. The Navy does what it can to promote domestic tranquillity. When family problems arise, there are places to turn to. An ombudsman is available at every naval station to interface between the Navy and families. The wives of submariners are a close-knit, mutually supportive group.

Despite the problems, despite the hardships, these men genuinely like being submariners. They like feeling they are personally important to the ship's mission. Many seem to imply, "See how tough this duty is, and I *volunteered*. I'm tough, too. I can take it, and I keep coming back for more."

They also like being part of a team. To operate a submarine demands teamwork of the highest order. But it goes beyond that. The crew of a submarine is an archetypal example of male bonding, and male bonding eases the hardship, soothes the loneliness, and makes the unthinkable bearable. The dangers seem less threatening because they are shared. The moral burden imposed by the lethal missiles aboard is diluted by sharing, and by fixing the responsibility elsewhere. A fire controlman, questioned about the ultimate consequences of his job, spoke in platitudes until his patience was exhausted, then snapped, "*We* don't fire the missiles. The *president of the United States* fires the damn missiles!"

2 | The Destruction of Her Country's Enemies

Submarines and submariners are both made in the New London, Connecticut, area and have been since 1900, when the Navy reluctantly decided to buy its first submarine. Nuclear submarines are built along the Thames River in Groton, Connecticut, at the Electric Boat Division of General Dynamics. Submariners are trained on the river nearby at the Naval Submarine Base. Submarines operate out of here, and the base provides a variety of special services to the submarine fleet. Some 15,000 sailors are stationed here, all either submariners or involved with submarines in some way. Submarines are what New London is all about. The launching of a new submarine is a joyous civic event.

Electric Boat built the Navy's first submarine in 1900 and has the design contract for the propulsion system of the

Seawolf class, the new generation of attack submarines. This is big business. The annual payroll at Electric Boat is more than $624 million.

Electric Boat built seventy-four submarines during World War II and supervised the building of twenty-eight others. It built the *Nautilus*, the first nuclear submarine, in the early 1950s. Since then, the company has designed fifteen of the eighteen classes of the Navy's submarines. It has built twenty-four of the thirty-eight Los Angeles–class attack submarines, and all of the Tridents.

Currently two classes of submarines are being built at Electric Boat, fast-attack submarines (SSNs) and ballistic-missile submarines (SSBNs). A fast-attack submarine is a tube of 2-inch-thick steel weighing 6,135 tons, 360 feet long with a 33-foot beam. It displaces 6,900 tons submerged and carries a crew of 142.

Ballistic-missile submarines, the Ohio-class Tridents, are 560 feet long (15 feet longer than the Washington Monument is high), measure 42 feet at the beam, displace 18,700 tons submerged, and carry a crew of 165.

Tridents, called boomers by submariners, are fitted with twenty-four ballistic missiles (SLBMs), which can be launched while submerged. Each missile is fitted with eight, and potentially twelve, nuclear warheads. A Trident can deliver a total payload of 19.2 megatons, 1,280 times the power of the atomic bomb that fell on Hiroshima. There were eight Tridents in the mid-1980s, carrying a total of 192 SLBMs with 1,536 warheads.

There are another twenty-eight ballistic-missile submarines in the older Lafayette, James Madison, and Benjamin Franklin classes, most of them built by Electric Boat. Collectively they have 5,472 nuclear warheads, a total deliverable explosive force of 403.2 megatons.

*The ballistic missile submarine Ohio, 560 feet long, rolls out of the assembly
building at Electric Boat Co.'s Groton, Connecticut yard.*

Beginning with the ninth Trident, the USS *Tennessee*
(SSBN-734), launched in December 1986, new SSBNs carry
the D-5 weapon system, an array of 6,000-mile SLBMs with
the accuracy and explosive power to hit and destroy the
hardest missile enforcements.

A ballistic submarine is a mobile missile silo. After leaving port, it proceeds to a secret point in the ocean where it
is on station, staying submerged there for sixty or seventy
days. Each SSBN has two crews, a blue and a gold, complete
from captain on down, which alternate tours at sea. This
arrangement gives the Navy full utilization of its SSBNs. To
meet demanding deployment schedules, crews fly to and
from SSBN bases. There is a short period when the crews
overlap, allowing the fresh crew to be briefed firsthand on
the status of all the equipment and systems aboard.

The Naval Submarine Base was founded in 1916, and every submariner, officer or enlisted man, who ever served aboard a Navy submarine learned his trade at the submarine school here. Other related commands share the 1,325-acre base: Submarine Group Two, comprised of three squadrons of fast-attack submarines; the submarine tender *Fulton;* the submarine rescue ship *Sunbird;* a number of schools offering training in specialized submarine skills; a hospital; the Submarine Medical Research Laboratory; the Naval Medical Underseas Institute; and a submarine museum.

Submarine officers come from three sources: the naval academy at Annapolis, the Naval Reserve Officer Candidate program (NROTC), and the Nuclear Propulsion Officer Candidate program (NUPOC), open to college juniors and seniors. Before being accepted, every candidate is inter-

An instructor at the submarine school in New London, Connecticut, demonstrates submarine trimming techniques.

viewed three times: a personal screening by a vice admiral and two technical interviews with senior engineering officers.

The NUPOC men go to Newport, Rhode Island, for Officer Candidate School, a four-month indoctrination into naval command. Upon graduation they are commissioned and join the Annapolis and NROTC officers for a year of advanced nuclear power training. It starts with twenty-six weeks of classroom training at the Nuclear Power School (NPS) at Orlando, Florida, and includes courses in advanced mathematics, physics, chemistry, electrical engineering, reactor theory, and thermodynamics, a total of 687 classroom hours.

Then comes twenty-four weeks of hands-on training at one of the Navy's three reactor training facilities in Idaho Falls, Idaho; Windsor Locks, Connecticut; and Ballston Spa, New York. After learning the systems and components of a nuclear plant, the officers train on a full-scale operating replica of a nuclear propulsion plant, and related systems.

Future submarine officers go to New London to attend the Naval Submarine School, where in thirteen weeks they will acquire the basic knowledge and skills needed by a submarine officer. Those who will serve on nuclear-propelled aircraft carriers and cruisers go to the Surface Warfare Officer School.

All officers aboard a submarine except the supply officer are specialists in nuclear propulsion. Some authorities believe this concentration on engineering does not produce effective submarine captains. Tom Clancy, the author of the submarine thriller *The Hunt for Red October,* says:

> Agreement in the submarine community—in private—is almost universal, the Royal Navy produces better commanding officers. Those aspiring to command are trained to one thing: operate the submarine and hit targets. The Royal

Navy's engineers are not allowed to command. The American system requires that a submarine officer spend too much time in the engine room. A submarine is not an excuse to build a nuclear reactor. A submarine is a weapon of war whose only purpose is the destruction of her country's enemies.

Upon graduation from submarine school, an officer begins his apprenticeship aboard a submarine in one of several billets: damage control assistant, main propulsion assistant, electrical officer, or reactor controls assistant.

When the captain decides that the officer has completed his apprenticeship satisfactorily, usually after six to eight months, he invites the commodore of the sub group and two other officers aboard. They question the officer to make sure he is proficient in his duties. The commodore interviews him to make sure he has the proper mental attitude and motivation to be a career submarine officer. If he passes muster, the dolphin insignia is pinned on his uniform. All qualified submariners, officers and enlisted men, wear the dolphin insignia.

The officer now is a full lieutenant and ready for more responsibility. Possible assignments include: communicator, the officer responsible for the conduct and supervision of radio communications; first lieutenant, responsible for the operation and maintenance of the ship's deck and the maintenance of the external hull; sonar officer, responsible for the conduct and supervision of underwater search; missile and missile fire control officer, responsible for operating, maintaining, and targeting missiles; torpedo and torpedo fire control officer, with similar responsibilities for torpedoes; and launching officer, responsible on SSBNs for the missile launcher subsystem. A knowledge of all these assignments is a prelude to command.

As an officer progresses, the Navy moves him around to broaden his background. After a tour of sea duty, he may be an instructor in one of the specialized schools or on the staff of a submarine group, then go to sea on a different class of submarine. If he earned his dolphins on a fast-attack submarine, he'll be assigned to a boomer.

All dream of commanding their own submarine. Those who make it are commanders in their middle or late thirties who have served as executive officers. A prerequisite to command is graduation from Prospective Commanding Officer (PCO) School.

A submarine captain serves one or, in exceptional instances, two three-year tours, then moves on to other command duties. It's not that captains burn out; their command time is limited by the number of qualified officers waiting to take their place.

Like submarine officers, enlisted submariners are an elite group. To qualify for enlisted nuclear training a young man must be between seventeen and twenty-five, a high school graduate, and score high on Navy aptitude tests. Beyond the normal medical standards, he must have normal color vision and be free of any congenital ailment, even acute acne. Submarine duty no longer has a special height limitation; submariners may be as tall as six feet six, the limit for all Navy personnel.

Every nuclear field recruit spends eight weeks of basic training at Orlando learning what the Navy is all about. Then he goes to one of the three specialty schools— mechanical, electrical, or reactor operator—for thirteen to thirty weeks.

For those who will become qualified nuclear operators, the next step is the Nuclear Power School for twenty-four weeks learning the theory and operation of a nuclear propulsion plant. The subjects, most taught at college level, include mathematics, physics, chemistry, heat transfer and fluid flow, reactor principles, reactor plant technology, and radiological fundamentals.

This is a demanding course, comparable to the one given to officers at their Nuclear Power School, and enlisted men of exceptional promise are encouraged to apply for either Annapolis or the NROTC program. Graduates of the enlisted men's Nuclear Power School go next to a nuclear power training unit (NPTU) to spend twenty-six weeks qualifying as a propulsion plant operator on a land-based prototype reactor plant.

Most NPTU graduates then go to submarine school, the others to nuclear-powered surface ships. However, not all enlisted submariners are graduates of NPTU. Sonarmen, radiomen, torpedomen, and cooks, for example, are trained in specialized schools and learn the basics of nuclear propulsion while aboard submarines.

A psychological screening test is given to determine a candidate's ability to cope with the stresses of life aboard a nuclear submarine. The test is designed to detect potential problems: suicidal tendencies, persecution complexes, latent paranoia, claustrophobia. If any abnormality is indicated, a Navy psychiatrist will evaluate the candidate to determine if he should be allowed to continue submarine training.

The test was developed and refined over the years by the Submarine Medical Research Laboratory. It has a staff of eighty, a quarter of whom are Ph.D.s. The commander, Captain Claude A. Harvey, is a Navy doctor who has spent time on seventeen different submarines in the course of his research.

"Very few are rejected from submarine school for psychological problems," Captain Harvey explains. "The reason is that a lot of self-screening has taken place before the man gets here. Someone who is terrified of being shut up in a small space doesn't volunteer for submarine duty. And rarely does someone with a psychiatric disorder have the motivation to get through the intensive training that precedes submarine school. Submarine volunteers almost invariably want to prove something to themselves, and they possess a high degree of self-discipline.

"It's hard to be on a submerged submarine for a long time," he says, "but not that much harder than being at sea for a comparable time on a surface ship. Go below decks on a cruiser or a carrier, the space is almost as confining as on a submarine. The only difference is that the man can't go up on deck to get away from it all and feel the sun on his face."

A submariner, he explains, is kept busy, usually with intellectually demanding tasks. "When he has finished his watch, he's tired, and because he's tired he's less apt to react negatively to his environment. We're herd animals. If we see others adapting, we're more apt to adapt ourselves. The senior petty officers, the old hands, if you will, have a calming effect on those who are making their first patrol.

"As to the length of time they are submerged, surprisingly, it doesn't make a difference," he says. "If a man is going to be disturbed by being on a submarine, he'll be disturbed quite early on. In other words, tension doesn't seem to build; any pressures in that direction are mitigated by the adaptive process he is undergoing. A man suffering a breakdown aboard a submarine is as rare as, say, a man with a ruptured appendix."

When nuclear submarines were first built, the Submarine Medical Research Laboratory ran an experiment, Project Hideout, to determine how long a crew could stay submerged. A crew, accompanied by laboratory observers, went aboard a docked submarine and performed their duties without coming out, just as if they were at sea. The experiment was called off after sixty days because all the food had been eaten. The crew was tired, but no psychological problems had surfaced.

What is the ideal personality for a submariner? The answer, apparently, is that there is none. Captain Harvey explains: "One would think that Type A personalities would make the best submariners. Full of energy, outgoing, take-charge guys. But in World War II, when a submarine would be taking a terrific pounding from depth charges, the lights out, filled with diesel fumes, the Type As didn't fare too well. They burned out, became phlegmatic. It was the Type Bs, the quiet, introspective men, who took charge and did the things that had to be done.

"It doesn't sound very scientific to say that we need all types of personalities—normal personalities—aboard a submarine, but it's true. Scientifically proven, at least to the Navy's satisfaction."

The crew of a ballistic-missile submarine has a particular psychological burden, the knowledge that they may someday have to rain destruction on helpless cities. This is an awesome responsibility for young men to live with.

"The men talk among themselves about this," Captain Harvey says. "Certainly it is on their minds. But they sincerely believe that they represent a deterrent to nuclear warfare, not a provocation. The psychological protection they employ is to believe they never will have to do it—and they are almost certainly correct. If an SSBN ever fires, she will have failed in her job. The Navy will have failed in its job.

"There's something else that should be understood about SSBNs. Any command to fire must come encoded by radio. Several officers would be involved in decoding the message. All must agree that an order to fire has been given, and all must agree to fire. The ship must be brought to the proper depth for firing. All this involves so many officers and men that there is no way a missile can be launched by a crazed captain, or by a few crazed crewmen, for that matter."

The laboratory is currently working on several projects. One is developing programs to assist submarine pharmacist mates in making diagnoses. Another explores ways to help sonarmen and radarmen read the displays on their machines more accurately. This is a subject close to Captain Harvey's heart.

"After the *Vincennes* [a U.S. cruiser] shot down the [Iranian] airliner in the Persian Gulf, much criticism centered on radar operators not being able to properly read what is on their screen—no way to tell the good guys from the bad guys. Let me assure you that considerable time and money goes into making operators more proficient, and making the displays easier to read. The funding for our project, for example, is in excess of a million a year."

The nearby Naval Underseas Medical Institute has an enviable reputation for applied research. Among its accomplishments: international use of the color orange for life jackets and buoys; the Falant Test, the definitive process for determining normal color vision; and the red lighting aboard submarines used to enhance night vision. The institute now is experimenting with very low-intensity white light to facilitate chart reading without impairing night vision.

Near the institute on the bank of the river is the New London area's major tourist attraction, the Nautilus Memorial/Submarine Force Library & Museum, attracting more than a quarter of a million visitors a year. They approach the museum through a bronze arch, a replica of the hull ring of an Ohio-class submarine, a forty-three-foot reminder of just how big ballistic submarines are. On the grounds are some vintage submarines, including Simon Lake's *Explorer* and a Japanese midget submarine.

In the entrance hangs an eleven-foot model of Jules Verne's fanciful *Nautilus*. Inside are working periscopes, a World War II control room, and a wall of models depicting the development of the submarine. Two mini theaters show short movies depicting the history of the submarine and the career of the real *Nautilus,* decommissioned in 1980 and moved here in 1985. Visitors may go below on the *Nautilus* and tour the control room and crew's quarters. The first of the nuclear submarines looks surprisingly dated, resembling the submarines of World War II as much as it does the submarines of today.

3 | Assassination at the Bottom of the Sea

Since the dawn of time, man apparently has dreamed of exploring the ocean depths. Voyages to wondrous underwater kingdoms are a recurring mythological theme. Herodotus, Aristotle, and Pliny the Elder all wrote about attempts to build various sorts of submersible vessels.

Alexander the Great may have been the first submariner, some 333 years before the birth of Christ. Numerous early histories described him submerging in some sort of glass barrel and seeing sea monsters and other fantastic sights. *Alexandre le Grand au Moyen-Age,* an ancient French treatise, noted, "He entered into a glass case covered with asses' skins, that had a door that could be made fast closed with chains and a ring. Upon descending he took with him such food as was necessary, and two friends for company."

A medieval woodcut depicts Alexander the Great being lowered in a primitive diving bell—the first underwater exploration, circa 333 B.C.

A millennium and a half after Alexander, *Salman and Morolf,* a German poem circa 1200, sang of a diving boat built of leather with a long tube supplying air used to slip beneath enemy ships. The thirteenth-century scientist Roger Bacon wrote of an amazing "warlike machine . . . which being almost wholly submerged, would run through the water." Leonardo da Vinci, credited with inventing the airplane, the tank, and other devices of war, claimed to have created a submarine as well, but he deliberately left no description or sketches, explaining, "I do not publish or divulge on account of the evil nature of men who practice assassination at the bottom of the sea."

Mother Shipton, the famous English prophetess, foresaw the modern submarine: "Under water men shall walk, shall ride, shall sleep, shall talk."

Sir Francis Bacon (1561–1626) reported, "We have heard it said that they have invented another machine, like a little ship, by the aid of which man can travel below the water for a considerable distance." No corroborating evidence survives, however.

Tales of early submarines abound, but the first detailed description appeared in a 1578 treatise, *Inventions and Devices,* written by an Englishman, William Bourne: "It is possible to make a shippe or boate that may goe under the water unto the bottome, and so come up again at your pleasure."

Bourne's plan called for a boat-shaped wooden hull, decked over and sealed watertight. Leather bags built into the bilges acted as ballast tanks, admitting seawater through holes in the hull. As the bags filled, the vessel submerged. By squeezing the water out of the bags, the operator resurfaced. A hollow mast provided fresh air. There was no indication how the boat was propelled, but Bourne solved the basic problem of a submarine: the control of buoyancy. And he sensed the shape of things to come, promoting his book as "very necessary for all generals and captains, or leaders of men as well by sea or by land."

The first man to build a workable submarine was Cornelius Van Drebbel, a Dutch physician. He amazed London in 1620 by submerging to a depth of twelve feet in his oar-powered boat and rowing across the Thames. But Van Drebbel apparently was unaware of Bourne's design. There was no way to control the buoyancy of Van Drebbel's vessel, and it took constant hard rowing to keep it submerged. He did interest James VI in his submarine, reportedly taking the monarch for a test drive.

Neither Bourne nor Van Drebbel specified what purpose their submarines would serve. In 1653 a submarine specifically planned for warfare was built at Rotterdam by a Monsieur de Son, who had a childlike faith in his creation. He boasted that it "doeth undertake in one day to destroy an hundred ships," further claiming that his boat would have the speed of a bird and be immune to fire, storm, and bullets, "unless it please God." The vessel was a seventy-two-foot catamaran with a clockwork engine that proved inadequate for its task. Problems of propulsion would plague submarine designers for centuries.

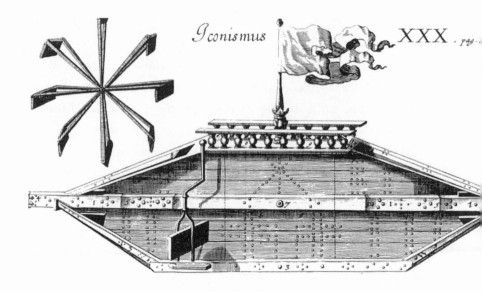

De Son's submarine, built in Rotterdam in 1653 but never tested.

There are numerous reports of crude submarines being built in the next century but little hard evidence. For example, Peter the Great of Russia ordered a submarine to be built. It was launched in 1729, during the reign of his son, Peter II, but nothing else is known.

The first recorded submarine fatality occurred on June 20, 1774. John Day, an English ship's carpenter, converted a sloop to a makeshift submarine by incorporating an air chamber and waterproofing. Day used large boulders hung from external ring bolts as detachable ballast. On his second dive something went wrong and the vessel sank in Plymouth Sound. An eyewitness report said, "She sank and Mr. Day descended with her into perpetual night."

At the start of the American Revolution, David Bushnell, a brilliant young Yale graduate, felt that a submarine might be able to help break the British naval blockade of New York City. He built a submarine, the *Turtle,* which looked like an enormous pineapple grenade. It had refinements that wouldn't be seen on a submarine again for many decades—a snorkel breathing apparatus, a depth gauge, and a detachable explosive charge with a time fuse.

Bushnell put the *Turtle* through a series of tests. Everything seemed satisfactory, but the operator, Bushnell's brother, became ill after submerging for some time. No connection was made between his malady and his prolonged submersion. Bushnell needed to find and train another operator. The Continental Army provided three volunteers, and one of them, Ezra Lee, is credited with carrying out the first submarine war mission in history.

It came as night fell on September 6, 1776. Two rowboats towed Lee and the *Turtle* down the Hudson River. Near where the British squadron was anchored off

Bushnell's Turtle, *the first American submarine (1776).*

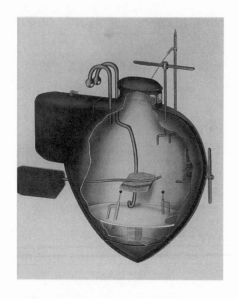

A modern schematic drawing of the Turtle.

Governor's Island, the boats slipped their tow and the current carried the little submarine down the river. Suddenly Lee saw he was drifting past the enemy fleet, and it took him two hours to work back upstream. Lee submerged under the hull of the British flagship, the sixty-four-gun *Eagle*, but repeatedly failed to attach the explosive charge to its copper-plated hull. He gave up when the sky started to lighten and headed upstream, the tide now in his favor. A British guard boat spotted him and gave chase. Lee set the time fuse and cut loose the explosive charge. The blast distracted the British boat, allowing the *Turtle* to float down the river to safety. The British fleet scattered. The primitive submarine had given the British something to think about.

The *Turtle* is believed to have made two other unsuccessful attacks on British ships. After the war it was being transported aboard a ship that ran aground on a reef and was lost to the sea. Bushnell's submarine received a fitting epitaph. In a letter to Thomas Jefferson, George Washington described the boat as an "effort of genius." But the government wasn't interested in buying Bushnell's submarine. Another 120 years would pass before the American Navy would take the submarine seriously.

A similar submarine reportedly was in operation during the War of 1812. The seventy-four-gun British ship *Ramillies* reported in July 1813 that it was attacked by a "diving boat" that penetrated the copper sheathing on its bottom, but apparently was unable to attach an explosive charge.

Robert Fulton, the Yankee inventor, was interested in submarines. An ardent pacifist, he saw the submarine as a way to destroy navies and rid the world of repressive armaments. After producing a workable design, Fulton sailed to France. He believed the French Revolution was a great force for freedom, and he wanted to place his submarine in its service.

On December 13, 1797, he approached the Directory, the committee that ruled France, offering a "mechanical engine" to destroy the British Navy, which was then blockading the French coast. Fulton proposed building the submarine at his own expense; for every British ship it sank he would be paid 4,000 francs per gun. The nearly bankrupt Directory decided that if the submarine sank even one British warship the Directory would sink, too.

The Directory negotiated the price down but refused to grant naval status to the submarine crew; if captured they could be hanged as pirates. Discouraged, Fulton tried unsuccessfully to find Dutch backing. Two years later he was back in France, negotiating with Napoleon Bonaparte. The British still blockaded France, and Napoleon welcomed the idea of a new weapon. He gave Fulton 10,000 francs to build the submarine.

The submarine, christened the *Nautilus,* was launched in 1801. Cylindrical in shape, it had a copper hull covering iron frames, a conning tower, and diving planes. Propelled by a hand-operated screw, the *Nautilus* used a kite-shaped sail while on the surface. On the Seine opposite the Hôtel des Invalides, the submarine descended to twenty-five feet.

Fulton's Nautilus, *which could sail on or below the surface (1801).*

Sea trials were scheduled off the port of Brest, but the Maritime Prefect of Brest decided he could not sanction trials for what he regarded as an inhumane instrument of war. The situation disintegrated into arguments over money, denouncements of Fulton as a charlatan, and French admirals publicly calling the submarine an unsound idea. More to the point, a cease-fire was being negotiated with Britain, and a submarine could only complicate matters. Napoleon withdrew his support.

In 1804 Fulton went to England and was received by Prime Minister William Pitt, who appointed a committee to investigate whether Britain should purchase the American's submarine. In a demonstration, Fulton blew up a Navy brig. The Royal Navy's response was a classic example of what happens when a conservative establishment is presented with a challenging idea. Pitt was called "the greatest fool that ever existed to encourage a mode of warfare which those who commanded the sea did not want, and which, if successful, would deprive them of it." Fulton abandoned the submarine for the steamboat.

An English smuggler and adventurer named Captain Johnson reportedly built a submarine in 1820 to rescue Napoleon from his St. Helena imprisonment for a reward of 40,000 pounds sterling. Napoleon died before the submarine was ready. Johnson then tried to get France to purchase five submarines, but nothing came of it.

War broke out between Denmark and Prussia in 1850, and the Danish fleet blockaded the Prussian coast. Wilhelm Bauer, a Bavarian artillery sergeant, designed a submarine, the *Brandtaucher* (fire diver), a sheet-iron rectangular tank propelled by a handwheel. Water ballast lowered buoyancy, and the diving angle was changed by moving a heavy weight back and forth inside the submarine. The hull tended to develop leaks when submerged.

The maiden voyage was a success, and the Danes withdrew their ships from Kiel. But a month later, diving in fifty feet of water in Kiel Harbor, the submarine's stern plating collapsed. Bauer coolly told his two crewmen to let the boat flood so that air pressure would force open the hatches. Five hours later they reached the surface, the first to escape a damaged submarine.

Bauer went to Britain during the Crimean War to sell a submarine. There was talk of "Lord Palmerston's submarine," but all that is known is that Scott Russell, a well-known British naval architect, produced a design for a submarine after several meetings with Bauer, and that Prime Minister Henry Palmerston approved funding a prototype. Apparently it was never built.

Bauer went to Russia in 1855 with a commission to build a fifty-two-foot submarine called *Seeteufel* (sea devil). During the coronation ceremonies of Tsar Alexander II, the submarine submerged with musicians aboard. They struck up the Russian national anthem and it was heard faintly by the guests ashore—a demonstration of how well and how far sound travels underwater.

French interest revived, and in 1858 the Ministry of Marine invited proposals for a submarine to protect the coast. Charles Brun was given a contract and built the 140-foot *Plongeur.* It incorporated a number of innovations, including reservoirs for compressed air that both expelled water from the ballast tanks and drove a four-cylinder engine.

What was lacking now was a proper submarine weapon. The *Plongeur* carried a spar torpedo, a canister of explosives on the end of a pole that was detonated by poking it against the side of an enemy ship. It would prove to be counterproductive.

In the American Civil War, the Confederacy built small vessels called "Davids" to attack the Goliath-like Union warships blockading southern ports. Davids were torpedo boats that traveled very low in the water, submerging for brief periods with only the superstructure visible above the water.

The first David was swamped by the wake of a passing steamer but was raised and put back in action. Off Charleston, South Carolina, on October 5, 1863, it rammed its spar torpedo into the Union ironclad *New Ironsides,* causing extensive damage but killing most of the David's crew.

Another submarine, the *H. L. Hunley,* named after her designer, was built of steel boilerplate and resembled a cigar. It was forty feet long and only forty-two inches in diameter, and the crew came aboard through hatches at either end. The *Hunley* also was easily swamped, sinking three times in sea trials with a loss of twenty-three crewmen.

On the night of February 17, 1864, the *Hunley,* commanded by Lieutenant George E. Dixon and carrying a crew of eight, crossed Charleston Harbor under cover of darkness. Spotting the Union fleet, Dixon chose the new 1,264-ton *Housatonic* as his target.

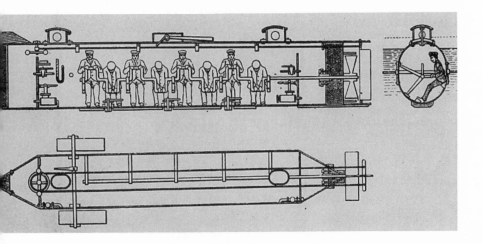

The Confederate ship Hunley, *the first successful attack submarine, which sank along with its first (and only) target (1864).*

The deck officer on the *Housatonic* caught sight of the *Hunley,* but before the ship could get underway the submarine was alongside. The thirty-foot projecting spar, supporting the canister of gunpowder, exploded on contact with the frigate, just forward of the main mast on the starboard side, abreast of the magazine. The *Housatonic* lifted bodily out of the water, then settled rapidly by the stern, the first ship ever sunk by a submarine.

Sunk, too, was the *Hunley* with all hands. It simply disappeared. It is believed that if there had been some way to detonate the spar torpedo from inside with the hatch sealed, it might have survived.

The Hunley Returns

Although the exact cause of the sinking of the Hunley remains a mystery, its whereabouts are not. In 1995, a group led by author Clive Cussler located the Hunley at the mouth of Charleston Harbor, in about 30 feet of water and buried under some three feet of silt. A five-year effort to raise the Hunley ensued, with contributions coming from Cussler as well as the U.S. Government and the state of South Carolina. At last, in August, 2000, a recovery team headed by Robert Neyland, the chief underwater archaeologist for the US Navy, brought the Hunley to the surface for the first time in 136 years. Restoration is expected to take at least several years. "The Hunley is an international treasure," said restoration expert Maria Jacobsen. "It's the first—the grandmother of all modern submarines."

Early in the war, another Confederate submarine turned up in Philadelphia. Harbor police stumbled on a "submarine monster" tied up at an island in the Delaware River. According to Robert F. Burgess's *Ships Beneath the Sea: A History of Subs and Submersibles,* the *Philadelphia Evening Bulletin* on May 17, 1861, reported:

> Never since the first flush of the bombardment of Fort Sumter, has there been an excitement in the city equal to that which was caused . . . by the capture of a mysterious vessel which was

said to be an infernal machine, which was to be used for all sorts of treasonable purposes, including the trifling pastime of scuttling and blowing up government men-of-war. For a few days past the police have had their attention directed the movements, not of a "long, low, black schooner", but of an iron submarine boat, to which very extraordinary abilities and infernal propensities were attributed.

The owner was Brutus de Villeroi, a Frenchman who had been trying to sell the submarine to the Union Navy. The seizure was a publicity break. The commandant of the Philadelphia Navy Yard examined the submarine and was impressed. A few months later de Villeroi wrote to President Lincoln to press his case. His letter concluded, "With a few such boats maneuvered each one by about a dozen men and the most formidable fleet can be annihilated in a short time."

De Villeroi was awarded a contract, and his *Alligator* was launched April 30, 1862. It saw no action, although some experts believed that it could have "destroyed, or at least rendered harmless" the Confederate ironclad *Merrimack* at Hampton Roads. The *Alligator* sank while under tow off Cape Hatteras on April 2, 1863.

Another Union submarine, nicknamed the *Intelligent Whale,* also was star crossed. Thirty-nine men drowned during sea trials. Designed by Oliver Halstead, the boat apparently had promise, except for the all-too-common tendency to be easily swamped.

The periscope was developed during the Civil War, but for ironclads, not submarines. The *Monitor Osage* used a periscope to locate a Confederate cavalry unit taking cover on the high banks of the Red River in Arkansas.

In 1866 an Englishman, Robert Whitehead, invented the self-propelled torpedo (the word *torpedo* comes from the

Latin for electric eel, *Torpedo electricus*). The Whitehead torpedo was used on surface ships for decades before a submarine capable of using it would be developed.

The man who almost singlehandedly created the modern submarine was a stubborn, idiosyncratic man who dreamed of freeing his native Ireland from British rule. He was born John Phillip Holland on February 24, 1841, in Liscannor on the Irish coast, and as a boy he was plagued with ill health. At seventeen, he took the vows of the teaching order of the Irish Christian Brothers. He soon found another passion, the Irish Revolutionary Brotherhood, dedicated to the cause of Irish freedom. Swept up in clandestine activities, he continued to teach because he needed the money.

Holland had a restless, curious mind and a knack for science. He decided that a submarine might attack the British fleet and tip the balance of power in Ireland's favor. He designed a submarine, but couldn't get it built. In 1873 he sailed for Boston to join his family.

No one in America was interested in his submarine, and he resumed teaching in Paterson, New Jersey, while refining his design. He wanted to work with other submarine designers but couldn't. According to Richard K. Morris's *John P. Holland, 1841–1914*, Holland later wrote:

> The development of vessels of this type was hindered by the secrecy maintained by everyone who had any knowledge of their design. Governments guarded the particulars of their experiments in order to preserve for themselves the advantage conferred by a successful submarine boat, and the results of individual efforts were just as carefully hidden to prevent the competition of other inventors. As each designer was thus compelled to face the problem without the knowledge of what had been accomplished by his prede-

cessors, he had to discover for himself the main requirements of a submarine vessel, and to foresee and provide
against difficulties.

But working alone might have been an advantage.
Holland was free of the mistakes of the past.

The Fenian Brotherhood, a large, fiercely militant force
for Irish freedom, became enchanted with Holland, and its
newspaper *Irish World* launched an appeal for funds to build
his submarine. Money poured in from the Irish-American
community. Prospective backers gathered at Coney Island to
watch Holland demonstrate a thirty-inch model of his submarine; they liked what they saw and opened their purses.
The Albany Iron Works in Paterson built Holland's submarine: a lozenge-shaped craft, 14½ feet long and 2½ feet high,
weighing 2¼ tons, and costing $4,000.

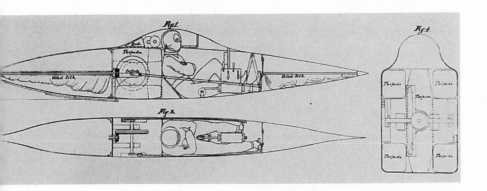

Submarine pioneer John Holland's first design, 1878.

The submarine was taken to the edge of the Passaic River. Reportedly someone on a nearby bridge looked down and said, "I see the Professor has built a coffin for himself." In the water the submarine settled rapidly and sank. Holland had miscalculated. The boat was designed for salt water; the Passaic River was fresh water, making a critical difference in buoyancy.

Adjustments were made within the hour and the boat floated properly, but now the two-cylinder gas engine wouldn't start. Holland spent weeks adapting the engine to steam. A launch generated steam and passed it through a rubber hose to the submarine's engine.

The launch, carrying a group of influential Fenians, chugged off down the river to an area free of other craft. Holland was in a space forty-six inches long and about twenty-four inches high with his head poking up into a sealed conning tower. He flooded the two ballast tanks and pushed the lever that controlled the diving rudders. Small tanks forward and aft were left empty to provide a slight positive

Turn-of-the-century boys' magazines fed the mania for submarines, like this triple-decker from 1892.

buoyancy to bring the craft to the surface in an emergency. The submarine submerged to a depth of twelve feet, reappearing safely a short distance away. Later Holland stayed submerged for an hour.

The trial runs demonstrated Holland's grasp of the principles of buoyancy and stability. Working alone, he had surpassed the work of earlier submarine designers. The Fenians agreed to fund another "wrecking boat." Holland turned his full attention to submarine design.

In 1879 the Fenians put up $23,000 for another submarine, the *Fenian Ram*, thirty-one feet long, six feet wide, and propelled by a gasoline engine. A freak accident during sea trials foundered the *Fenian Ram,* and it cost the backers $3,000 to have the boat raised. The trials dragged on, and the backers ran out of patience. They broke into the shipyard and towed the submarine away. They attempted to use the *Fenian Ram* themselves, finally giving up. Holland now had lost interest. "I'll let her rot on their hands," he said. The *Fenian Ram* was never in the water again.

Near bankruptcy, Holland tried to sell a submarine to the Navy Department. To make ends meet, he took a job as a draftsman at the Pneumatic Gun Company, where he met Captain Edmund L. Zalinski, an Army ordnance expert. The captain had a new "dynamite gun" and thought it should be mounted on a submarine. He could only afford a wooden submarine, however, and Holland reluctantly agreed to build it. Launched in 1885, it was an absolute failure. Holland later complained that the Zalinski boat set his career back ten years. Whatever the reason, Holland disappeared from the scene for more than a decade. Meanwhile submarine history was being made by, of all people, an English curate.

4 | *There, Sir! That Is the Perfection of Vessels!*

George William Garrett, the son of a Manchester, England, vicar, was admitted to Trinity College in Dublin at seventeen, and passed all the first-year examinations in his first week. Science was his first love, and after graduation he was appointed an assistant master at the Manchester Mechanics Institute. There he earned certificates in science, art, physical geography, geology, mathematics, and higher chemistry. To placate his father, Garrett also studied theology, and in 1873 he was ordained as curate. His primary interest, though, was submarine design.

After Garrett returned from a voyage around the world in 1877, the Russo-Turkish War broke out. He was intrigued when Russian torpedo boats were thwarted by Turkish harbor-defense nets. He felt that a submarine could have gone under the nets.

Garrett invented a self-contained breathing suit, the forerunner of today's scuba. Demonstrating it for the French Ministry of Marine, he stayed below the surface of the Seine for thirty-seven minutes, but the French weren't interested in breathing suits. They wanted submarines.

In 1878 Garrett was awarded a patent for "Improvements in and Appertaining to Submarine or Subaqueous Boats or Vessels for Removing, Destroying, Laying or Placing Torpedoes in Channels and other Situations, and for other Purposes." He founded his own firm that year, the Garrett Submarine Navigation and Pneumataphore Company, Ltd., financed by his father and some Manchester businessmen.

He built an experimental submarine, fourteen feet long and five feet in diameter. Instead of diving rudders for trimming the boat, Garrett borrowed an idea of William

George W. Garrett's Resurgam II *(1879), a steam-powered submarine that sank off the Welsh coast just after its first successful trials.*

Bourne's: a piston inside the boat that altered the boat's volume by drawing in or expelling water. A hand crank powered the boat. Gauntlets of greased leather installed in the hull enabled the pilot to reach outside and attach an explosive charge to a ship. Garrett christened his first submarine *Resurgam,* Latin for "I will rise again."

The submarine was criticized in the press and from the pulpit as an immoral weapon. In the prospectus for his company Garrett wrote, "As to the inventions being for murdering people—this is all nonsense. Every contribution made by science to improve instruments of war makes war shorter and, in the end, less terrible to human progress."

Resurgam performed well in sea trials, and Garrett built a larger boat and powered it with steam. It was cigar shaped, weighing close to thirty tons, and the hull could withstand pressure at a depth of nearly 150 feet. The submarine made two to three knots and could stay submerged for as long as steam could be produced. If the air inside the boat ran out, the crew could use Garrett's underwater breathing suit.

Resurgam II was launched on December 10, 1879, at Birkenhead. Garrett and a crew of two took the submarine down the Mersey River under her own power. Garrett planned to steam to Portsmouth to show his submarine to the wealthy Swedish arms manufacturer Thorsten Nordenfeldt. He purchased a small steam yacht, the *Elfin,* to tow the boat and serve as its escort.

As they headed west along the Welsh coast, a storm rose quickly and the towing hawser parted. Garrett watched *Resurgam II* flounder and sink, never to be recovered.

Garrett was in financial trouble, and Nordenfeldt seemed his only hope. They formed a partnership: Garrett had the submarine patent, Nordenfeldt the money. They built a submarine at Stockholm, the *Nordenfeldt No. 1,* and

sold it to Greece in 1883. Three years later Turkey bought
two submarines of the same design. The submarines had
problems—the boiler often leaked carbon monoxide into
the boat, and the ballast tanks made it rock—but they were
the first submarines to use the Whitehead automatic torpedo, which fired at a safe distance from the target.

Nordenfeldt and Garrett built three more submarines.
One participated in the Golden Jubilee Review of the British
Navy in 1887, attracting the attention of the visiting tsar, who
purchased it. But the submarine was damaged on the way to
Russia, and the tsar refused to honor the contract. The
other two submarines went unsold.

The partnership was dissolved. Nordenfeldt designed a
new submarine that no one wanted to buy, so he went back
to selling machine guns. Garrett emigrated to the United

*This Garrett and Nordenfeldt steam-powered submarine from the late 1880s had a
dinghy and smokestack, but no periscope.*

States and served as an Army engineer in the Spanish-
American War. In 1902, nearly destitute, he died in New
York at the age of fifty.

The major problem of submarines in those years was
propulsion. Neither steam nor the gasoline engine proved
satisfactory. Four designers in four countries worked independently on what would be the answer: electric-powered
submarines.

In New York, Josiah Tuck in 1884 built a thirty-foot,
electric-powered submarine called the *Peace Maker,* tested it
successfully, but couldn't find a buyer. In England, J. F.
Waddington, a shipbuilder, designed a thirty-seven-foot boat
in 1885 called the *Porpoise* and equipped it with a powerful
electric motor that enabled it to cruise 150 miles. The
Porpoise boasted two other significant innovations: hull
planes that automatically kept it horizontal when submerged, and two Whitehead torpedoes for armament. Also
in 1885, M. Goubet received a French patent for a submarine design incorporating an electric motor. The *Goubet I*
had a sixteen-foot hull made of bronze and cast as a single
piece. The two-man crew sat back to back, looking out of
windows in a small conning tower.

A young Spanish naval officer, Isaac Peral, came up with
the same answer to the propulsion problem. His 1886 design
included an electric motor powered by accumulator batteries. The Spanish Navy built the submarine, and it caught the
attention of the French. The leading French naval architect,
Dupuy de Lome, began designing a submarine incorporating Peral's idea; his associate, Gustave Zede, completed it
after de Lome's death.

The *Gymnote,* French for "eel," was built in 1887, sixty
feet long with a hull diameter of five feet ten inches, a
Whitehead torpedo mounted in its bow, and an electric

motor. The French rebuilt it several times to test new ideas. In 1896 a French competition drew some thirty designs for a 200-ton submarine with a surface range of one hundred miles. The winner was Maxime Laubeuf, and his design was the link between the early prototypes and the submarines of World War I.

Laubeuf's *Narval* used two propulsion systems: an electric motor for running submerged and steam for the surface. More important, the steam engine could recharge the accumulator batteries. It had a double hull in which fuel and water ballast could be stored, an innovation still in use today. The principal drawback was that it took the *Narval* twenty minutes to submerge, but the French Navy liked it well enough to order four more.

In America, John Holland followed reports of the progress of the French boats and grudgingly admitted that they had merit. "Totally sick and disgusted" with the U.S. Navy's lack of interest in his designs, he decided that some publicity might help. He published an article entitled "Can New York Be Bombarded?" describing the weaknesses of America's fleet and its coastal defenses, and how a few submarines could correct them.

The Navy took notice of the article and announced an open competition for a "submarine torpedo-boat." No designer met the specifications: fifteen knots on the surface, eight submerged—a performance level not attained until the late 1930s. Another competition was held with more realistic specifications. Holland won, but the Navy decided not to build his boat.

If the Navy wasn't fascinated with submarines, the public certainly was. Jules Verne's epic science-fiction fantasy *Twenty Thousand Leagues Under the Sea* was an international sensation in 1869. Designers worked feverishly to create

The Intelligent Whale, *Oliver Halstead's 26-foot hand-powered submarine whose failure in 1873 soured the U.S. Navy on submarines for years thereafter.*

their own version of a *Nautilus,* but most met with varying degrees of failure.

Many of the designs were bizarre: a two-part submarine, the underwater part with two columns supporting an above-water platform; a submarine resembling a corkscrew, which the designer claimed would enable it to twist through the water so swiftly it could cross the Atlantic in twenty-eight hours; one with pointed ends that theoretically could be dropped off while submerged, enabling the center section to float to the surface; another featuring hand-turned paddles and a rubber-band motor; a German design for a submarine shaped like "an ovoid bent askew" with a large picture window.

Germany had the most workable submarines, adaptations of Garrett and Nordenfeldt's design. They were large, more than one hundred feet in length, and attracted world-wide attention in the kaiser's 1890 fleet maneuvers.

Still in eclipse and broke, Holland took a menial job in a dredging company paying four dollars a day. In his spare time, he developed an idea for an airplane that could take off vertically. Nothing came of it, but it caught the attention of influential people. His luck began to change in 1893 when Grover Cleveland, a proponent of the submarine, regained the presidency.

Another submarine design competition was held. Holland won, and the Navy awarded him $200,000 to produce his design. The John P. Holland Torpedo Boat Company was formed, and a Baltimore shipyard was contracted to build the submarine, the *Plunger.* Contract specifications forced design concessions on Holland. The *Plunger,*

Holland's Plunger, *constructed under Navy design restrictions, never completed its sea trials (1897).*

launched in 1897, was so disappointing that its sea trials were called off. Holland then convinced the Navy to allow him to build a second submarine of his own design, and immediately started to construct his personal vision of a submarine.

The second submarine, *Holland VI*, launched the following year, was the forerunner of all modern submarines. It was fifty-three feet ten inches long with a diameter of ten feet three inches, displaced seventy-four tons submerged, with plating over a frame skeleton. A forty-five-horsepower gasoline engine gave it a speed of eight knots on the surface and also charged the accumulator batteries. A fifty-horsepower motor provided nearly the same speed underwater. The *Holland VI* had one tube and carried three Whitehead torpedoes and a new compensating system for maintaining the trim when a torpedo was fired. A system of clutches allowed the engine to charge the batteries while either running or standing—an innovation that would be used on submarines for more than fifty years.

Alan H. Burgoyne, a contemporary British authority, wrote, "Of this vessel perhaps more has been heard than of any other ship or boat in the world. She is the prototype of the latest submarine ordered by Great Britain and the American

John P. Holland, the father of the modern submarine, emerges from the USS Holland VI, *the first submarine purchased by the Navy, in 1900.*

government and is also, without doubt, the commencement of the 'really successful' submarine."

The submarine performed well in sea trials. On St. Patrick's Day 1898 it made a dive off Staten Island. Several days later the United States declared war on Spain. Assistant Secretary of the Navy Theodore Roosevelt, who monitored the submarine's sea trials, wrote Navy Secretary John D. Long, "I think that the Holland submarine boat should be purchased. Evidently she has great possibilities in her for harbor defense. Sometimes she doesn't work perfectly, but often does, and I don't think in the present emergency we can afford to let her slip."

Holland offered to take his submarine to Havana and blow up the Spanish fleet, but the Navy demurred. Building the submarine had stretched the resources of the Holland Boat Company to the breaking point. The company that supplied the batteries for the *Holland VI* stepped in and drove a hard bargain. The Holland Boat Company became the Electric Boat Company, and John Holland was no longer in financial control.

On April 11, 1900, the Navy finally accepted the *Holland VI*. The next year Holland built a larger boat, the *Fulton,* but the Navy didn't buy it and he sold it to Russia. Five Holland submarines were sold to Japan, although they apparently weren't used in the Russo-Japanese War of 1904–1905.

The U.S. Navy bestirred itself in 1903 and ordered six new Holland submarines—the *Adder, Grampus, Moccasin, Porpoise, Pike,* and *Shark.* These submarines formed the first United States Submarine Service. Other countries began buying submarines from Holland. Britain, though still committed to ruling the sea with surface ships, ordered five in response to France's submarine acquisitions.

Holland surpassed his *Holland VI* in 1906, building the 105-foot, 270-ton *Octopus*. The new boat carried a crew of fifteen and could make eleven knots on the surface, ten submerged. *Octopus* astounded observers by test-diving to a depth of 205 feet. The Navy was impressed but demanded that he test the *Octopus* against a new submarine, the *Simon Lake X*, named for Holland's closest competitor, a peppery young redhead who also knew the frustration of trying to sell to the Navy. The performance duel lasted ten days and received considerable attention in the press. The *Octopus* nosed out Lake's boat and was purchased.

The career of Simon Lake mirrored Holland's trials and tribulations. When he was eleven, Lake read of Captain Nemo and his submarine *Nautilus* in *Twenty Thousand Leagues Under the Sea,* and his life was changed forever. He reread the book countless times, and loved to quote from it, regaling his young friends with such passages as:

> No defects to be afraid of, for the double shell is as firm as iron; no rigging to attend to; no sails for the wind to carry away; no boilers to burst; no fire to fear, for the vessel is made of iron not of wood; no coal to run short, for electricity is the only mechanical agent; no collision to fear, for it alone swims in deep water; no tempest to brave, for when it dives below the water it reaches absolute tranquillity. There, sir! that is the perfection of vessels!

Lake grew to know Verne's *Nautilus* so well that he started to imagine improvements. He took a new interest in his schoolwork, and rose to the head of the class. He found that he had a flair for science, and he was determined to build a submarine someday. Two years out of school he patented a steering gear for high-wheeled bicycles, then a winding gear for oystermen, and a capping device for the canning industry, all the while working on designs for a submarine he called the *Argonaut*.

Learning of a Navy competition for submarine designs, Lake, then twenty-seven, went to Washington in 1893. His competitors were George Baker of Chicago and John Phillip Holland. Lake lost and barely had enough money left to get home to Atlantic Heights, New Jersey. But the experience left him more determined to build his submarine.

Failing to rise money, Lake planned a smaller boat, the *Argonaut Junior,* and members of his family put up the money to build it. When completed, the fourteen-foot submarine bore an uncanny resemblance to an old-time flatiron. The hull had flat sides; the conning tower was amidships, a wooden box with portholes. A unique feature was an air lock pressurized by compressed air to permit a diver to leave and reenter. *Argonaut Junior* also had two wheels forward mounted on an axle, and a third, smaller wheel at the stern. Despite its odd appearance, the boat performed well. Lake formed the Lake Submarine Company, capitalized at $2,500.

By selling shares, Lake was able to build the submarine he had originally planned. By coincidence, his *Argonaut I* was built in the same shipyard as the *Plunger,* and while the *Plunger* was a failure, Lake's boat did well in its sea trials. Lake took his boat to New York and invited newspaper reporters to take a cruise. The publicity stunt got a big play in the press, but proved of no help in attracting either buyers or more investors.

Seeking further publicity, Lake made a 2,000-mile tour of Chesapeake Bay, submerging as often as possible. It was the longest voyage of a submarine to date, and the first extended observation of marine life ever made.

On February 15, 1898, the battleship *Maine* was sunk in Havana, and Lake, like Holland, offered his submarine to the Navy, but was turned down. Lake saw another opportunity later that year when the Navy laid a minefield across

Simon Lake's Argonaut I *(1897) had large wheels that enabled it to crawl on the bottom of the sea. The* Argonaut *made a 2,000-mile journey along the bottom of Chesapeake Bay in the first extended observation of undersea marine life.*

Hampton Roads, a channel connecting the James and Elizabeth Rivers with Chesapeake Bay, apparently anticipating the Spanish fleet. Lake took the *Argonaut* under the minefield, carefully noting through a porthole how the field was laid out. He wrote the Navy about his escapade, including the details of the minefield, and pointed out that his submarine was capable of both laying and disarming mines. The Navy did not respond.

While returning to New Jersey, the submarine was caught in a severe sleet storm with towering waves. Lake lashed himself into the conning tower and shouted directions to his two crewmen below. The *Argonaut* made it, although more than a hundred ships were lost. Newspapers around the world reported the submarine's performance.

Even Jules Verne cabled congratulations. Lake always regarded this as one of the high points of his life.

Lake raised enough money to build a more conventional submarine—no wheels, no flat-sided hull, no portholes. Built in 1902, the *Protector* was a sixty-five-foot, 130-ton boat with a twin propulsion system similar to Holland's. *Protector* was the first submarine to mount a gun on its foredeck and to have a workable periscope, which Lake called an "omniscope."

A demonstration for the Navy aroused no interest, but the Army was impressed and ordered five. The Navy successfully lobbied to get the appropriation bill defeated, though, and Lake began looking to other countries for possible sales. Russia, at war with Japan, agreed to buy the *Protector* and five more of the same design. Lake and his crew went to Russia to show the tsar's Navy how to operate the boat.

No submarines saw action in the Russo-Japanese War, but Russia was enchanted with them and wanted to expand its underwater fleet. Lake built two submarines for Austria, then set up a joint operation with the Krupp armament makers in Germany. He neglected to protect his patents in Germany, however, and received no royalties.

Lake returned home and built the *Simon Lake X,* incorporating all he had learned from the *Argonaut* series and the *Protector.* The Navy turned it down after it was tested against Holland's *Octopus.* An angry Lake sold the boat to his old customer, Russia. Later, Congress took over the purchasing of submarines and commissioned Lake to build a submarine. However, the Navy's requirements were formidable:

> The Lake Company will build at its own expense a submarine which will be:
>
> Faster on the surface or under it than any boat now building, either in the United States or abroad.

It will have a greater radius of action, more powerful armament, eight torpedo tubes, safety features by which a man can escape when the boat is submerged, and facilities for planting mines and cutting cables.

It will do more than the United States Government has ever asked that any submarine do. If it does not do all that is claimed for it, the United States Government need never pay us a cent of money.

In response, Lake designed and built the *Seal,* a 161-foot, 400-ton boat, the largest built up to that time. It carried a crew of twenty-four and was armed with six torpedoes. On October 12, 1912, the Navy accepted the *Seal.* Simon Lake finally achieved the recognition in his own country he had craved for so long.

The last years of John Phillip Holland were unhappy. Others were reaping the profits from his superlative designs. He had a small income from early patents, but his bitterness over the loss of his company dulled his enthusiasm and ruined his health. He put aside submarines and again turned to aviation, writing a book, *How to Fly as a Bird.*

Holland died in a hospital in Newark on August 12, 1914, five days after the beginning of World War I. It probably would have pleased the old Fenian had he lived to see how submarines soon would bedevil the British.

5 | *Build More Submarines!*

When Gavrilo Princep assassinated Archduke Francis Ferdinand of Austria on June 28, 1914, none of the great powers was putting much stock in submarines. They built them because their traditional enemies built them, but victory at sea was the business of battleships and cruisers. These ships reigned supreme, in battle and in naval appropriations.

In 1901 Admiral Alfred von Tirpitz had told the Reichstag that the German Navy didn't need submarines, explaining, "We have no money to waste on experimental vessels. We must leave such luxuries to wealthier states like France and England." But when Russia purchased three submarines, Tirpitz changed his mind. The first submarine joined the German fleet in 1908.

By 1914 Germany had twenty-nine submarines, and both Britain and France had about twice that many. The major powers built their own submarines, Britain and France from modified John Holland designs, Germany from Simon Lake's design. German submarines had the advantage of a German invention, the diesel engine. Remarkably reliable, it produced no spark, and diesel oil was not as dangerous to have aboard a submarine as gasoline. Diesel engines gave U-boats, from the German *unterseeboot,* a range of 3,000 miles, which would work to Germany's advantage. By contrast, Britain and France developed shorter-range submarines: small, sturdy, and fast.

Despite this activity, not much thought had been given to how submarines would be used in time of war. The Hague Convention of 1899 codified the rules of civilized naval warfare, and it was assumed they applied to submarines. The rules said a warship was not to fire on an unarmed merchantman. To determine if a ship was carrying contraband, it would be ordered to stop and its papers examined. If the ship was trading with the enemy, it could be taken as a prize, or sunk after the crew were put aboard lifeboats. If the weather was bad, the crew would be taken aboard the warship.

But to stop a merchantman a submarine would have to surface, exposing itself to attack. A submarine crew was too small to spare men to oversee a prize ship. Nor was there room aboard a submarine to hold the crew of a merchantman. The Hague Convention did not address itself to these problems, perhaps assuming that submarines would concentrate on attacking warships.

The first wartime confrontation was conducted according to the Hague rules. Off the coast of Norway on October 20, 1914, the small British steamer *Glitra* was stopped by the

German submarine *U-17*. The crew was put in lifeboats, the sea cocks opened, and the *Glitra* went to the bottom, the first merchantman to be sunk by a submarine. In the first six months of the war, ten merchantmen were similarly sunk by U-boats. Their captains had been cautioned not to waste torpedoes.

But the primary objective of a submarine was to sink warships, not merchantmen. Shortly after war was declared, a British submarine, the *E-9,* slipped into the bight of Helgoland north of Wilhelmshaven in the North Sea and found the German cruiser *Hela* lying at anchor. Two Whitehead torpedoes sent her to the bottom. The *Hela* was the first warship to be sunk by a submarine's torpedoes since the *Housatonic* was dispatched by the Confederate *Hunley* in the Civil War.

In December 1914 another British submarine, the *B-11,* amazingly threaded its way through the Dardanelles minefields to the Sea of Marmara, sank the Turkish battleship *Messudiyeh,* and returned home safely despite a malfunctioning compass.

The U-boats also got in some early punches. The *U-21* sank the flotilla leader HMS *Pathfinder,* most of the crew going down with the ship.

Both British and German submarines experienced problems. British torpedoes ran beneath their targets; German submarines were plagued by mechanical breakdowns. The *U-15* broke down at sea, and while on the surface being repaired she was rammed and sunk by the cruiser HMS *Birmingham.* Another U-boat struck a British mine and went down with all hands. Both British and German warships accidentally fired on their own submarines.

Life aboard a World War I submarine was hard, whatever flag it flew. The average submarine was about 150 feet long, carrying three officers and a crew of thirty in varying degrees of discomfort. There were bunks for only half the crew, and the men slept in shifts. No matter how exhausted, everyone turned to when the claxon sounded, for the safety of the boat was at stake.

There was no refrigeration, and after a few days at sea only canned rations could be served. There were no bathing facilities. The toilet used air pressure to flush waste out of the submarine, a tricky business. If the water pressure outside the submarine exceeded that of the air pressure inside, a phenomenon occurred called "getting your own back."

Interiors were cramped. Moving from one part of a submarine to another was arduous. The interior could be brutally hot while the submarine traveled on the surface, bitterly cold submerged.

The smell inside defied description, a noxious mixture composed of the aroma of unwashed bodies, rotting food, excreta, fumes from the bilge, and smoke from the diesel on the surface or battery fumes submerged. No wonder American submariners called them "pig boats." Only dying on a submarine was worse than living on one.

But the submariners surmounted their hardships and were surprisingly effective. On September 22, 1914, the *U-9* singlehandedly sank three cruisers, the *Aboukir, Cressy,* and *Hague.* The British admiralty was shocked. An admiral said, "It is the German Fleet that now controls the North Sea!" The Grand Fleet hastily moved to the west coast of Scotland to wait until the antisubmarine defenses at its Scapa Flow base could be increased. Germany scored a strategic victory but did not exploit it.

Suddenly submarines were all the British could think about. "Build more submarines!" First Sea Lord Jackie Fisher urged Winston Churchill, first lord of the admiralty.

Shipyards sharply increased the construction of Holland-type submarines.

British submarines performed admirably. Two legendary captains, Noel Laurence and Max Horton, harassed German squadrons in the Baltic. Horton torpedoed eight destroyers off the Danish cost. During a battle between German and Russian ships, he slipped in unnoticed and damaged a German battleship with a torpedo.

Meanwhile Laurence also torpedoed a battleship. He spotted the entire German battle-cruiser squadron and fired once, striking the *Moltke,* damaging her severely. He eluded the escort destroyers and escaped. After his attack, the German squadron turned back from its planned attack on Riga, Latvia.

Germany put a price on Laurence's head, and Grand Admiral Prince Heinrich announced, "I regard the destruction of a British submarine as being at least as valuable as that of a Russian armored cruiser."

Under the Anglo-French alliance, most French submarines were stationed in the south of France, patrolling the Mediterranean and the Adriatic, alert for signs of the Austro-Hungarian fleet. The Austrians had a few submarines of their own, and one of them, the *XII,* torpedoed the French battleship *Jean Bart* in December 1914, inflicting severe damage.

Germany did not like the way the war was going. Admiral Spee's squadron was mauled in the South Atlantic; four German capital ships were sunk, with the loss of more than 2,200 men. The armed merchantmen were a disappointment. The army was bogged down on the Western Front. The high command pressed for unrestricted submarine warfare, but the kaiser worried about its effect on neutrals, particularly Italy and the United States.

The high command got its way. On February 4, 1915, Germany declared that a war zone existed around the British Isles; merchantmen found in the zone, including those of neutral nations, would be sunk without warning. Germany contended this was the only possible response to the Allied blockade of Germany, itself in violation of the accepted rules of war.

Germany had only twenty-nine U-boats, most of them old, yet in less than three months they were able to sink thirty-nine ships. Each month their total increased, as did the revulsion of the world to the U-boat campaign. Then Germany made a serious blunder.

In the early afternoon of May 7, 1915, Captain Schweiger of the *U-20* sent a torpedo into the *Lusitania*. Twenty minutes later the British liner was at the bottom with

The sinking of the Lusitania *(1915) by a German U-boat helped draw the United States into World War I.*

1,198 of its crew and passengers, many of whom were children. Among the victims were 128 Americans.

The sinking touched off a firestorm of protest. Germany claimed the *Lusitania* was carrying 173 tons of ammunition, and advertisements placed by the German government in New York newspapers had warned Americans of the danger. This rationale fell on deaf ears. The *Lusitania* became synonymous with German infamy.

Shipping losses to U-boats fell off in the wake of the *Lusitania* sinking, prompting Churchill to speak of "the failure of the German submarine campaign." British warships sank seven U-boats, and experiments with acoustic mines and depth charges were promising. In March 1915 the *U-8* was caught in the nets at Dover and sunk. A few days later the battleship *Dreadnought* rammed and sank the *U-12* commanded by Korvetten-Kapitan Weddigen, who had sunk the three British cruisers, and Britain had something to cheer about. The cheers were premature. The worst was yet to come.

On August 19 another British liner, the *Arabic,* was sunk by the *U-24* off Ireland. Among the dead were three Americans. The U.S. sharply protested, and within days Germany banned attacks on liners, sending its U-boats to the Mediterranean and the North Sea. But German shipyards continued to work overtime building U-boats; sixty-one were completed by the end of 1915.

The number of U-boats in service wasn't the number in combat. Five U-boats were needed to maintain a combat position: one on the position, another on its way home, a third on its way out, one being made ready for sea, and a fifth in dry dock. In *The Great War at Sea: 1914–1918* author Richard Hough summarizes a German Navy report: "The large amount of technical apparatus aboard a U-boat required very careful overhauling and repair on the return from an expedition; also, the damage due to the voyage or from enemy attacks had to be repaired. Generally speaking, after four weeks at sea a boat would need to lie in the dockyard for the same length of time for repairs."

U-boats soon were back in the Atlantic, and shipping losses increased dramatically. In January 1915 U-boats sank 32,000 tons of British shipping and 15,390 tons of French and neutral shipping. By March the total had risen to 80,700 tons; by May, 185,000. Germany now had a base at Bruiges in occupied Belgium, giving U-boats easy access to Atlantic shipping lanes.

Britain was feeling the pinch. In a way, so was America. The war economies of Britain and France had created profitable new markets for American munitions and increased orders for other products. But there was no profit if the ships carrying American merchandise were sunk.

The 1915 U-boat offensive prompted Britain to call up yachts, trawlers, and other craft, put guns aboard, and send them on submarine patrol. Destroyers escorted capital ships everywhere; there would be no more sitting ducks. But there simply was too much sea to patrol.

Smelling blood, the German Navy again urged unrestricted submarine warfare, claiming it would starve Britain out of the war in six months. The kaiser was tempted, but feared it would bring America into the war. A compromise was worked out. In the war zone enemy merchantmen were fair game; outside the zone they could be sunk without warning only if they were armed. Liners would be spared. The Navy reluctantly agreed, warning that U-boats would find these restrictions difficult.

The Navy was right. The renewed U-boat campaign began February 11, 1916, and less than a month later the *U(B)-29* torpedoed the French passenger steamer *Susan* in the English Channel. The *Susan* didn't sink, but many of its 380 passengers were killed or injured, including several Americans.

President Woodrow Wilson, through the State Department, told Germany that it must abandon "its present methods of submarine warfare against passenger and freight-carrying vessels" or face a break in diplomatic relations. The German response was to publicly call off the U-boat campaign, but the U-boats soon went back to their old tactics. The toll on Allied shipping again increased, exceeding a half million tons a month by the end of the year.

The British introduced "Q-ships," decoy vessels with concealed guns. A Q-ship would loiter in a likely area to lure a U-boat to the surface. When the Q-ship was accosted, most of the crew would abandon ship, leaving a secret gun crew behind. When the U-boat closed for an easy shot, the gun crew would open fire. The Q-ships sank a few U-boats at first, but never enough to justify their expense. The Allies also armed merchantmen; the U-boats responded by torpedoing merchantmen on sight.

Two effective antisubmarine devices came into service in 1916, the hydrophone and the depth charge. The hydrophone gave the Allies a way to detect the presence of submerged U-boats; the depth charge, 300 pounds of explosives rigged to go off at a predetermined depth, proved capable of destroying them. In July 1916 the *Salmon*, equipped with hydrophones, became the first patrol to sink a U-boat with depth charges.

In 1916 a curiosity arrived in Baltimore, the cargo submarine *Deutschland*. Owned by the German Lloyd Lines, the 315-foot-long submarine had crossed the Atlantic in only sixteen days carrying 600 tons of cargo. Simon Lake, who had envisioned cargo-carrying submarines himself, went to

Baltimore to welcome the *Deutschland,* only to find that it had infringed on many of his patents. He threatened to sue but was placated with promises of postwar contracts. The *Deutschland* returned home loaded with nickel, tin, and rubber, much to the annoyance of the British.

Germany felt that the visit was a propaganda victory, and a second cargo submarine, the *Bremen,* set out for Newport, Rhode Island, but was sunk by a mine off the Orkneys. The *Bremen'*s escort, the *U-53,* proceeded to lie off the American coast, sinking a merchantman within sight of the Nantucket lightship.

By early 1917 Germany was convinced that America soon would enter the war, and that its only hope was to force Britain to sue for peace. The German Fleet had narrowly escaped destruction at the battle of Jutland in May 1916 and was no longer a factor in the war. But new submarines were coming into service, and the average number at sea had risen from ten in mid-1914 to nearly forty. Unrestricted submarine warfare was resumed.

At first the gamble paid off. In April 1917, U-boats sank nearly one of every four ships entering the war zone, a total of 800,000 tons. In February and March of 1916, 1,149 ships had arrived in British ports; a year later, 300. Merchantmen were being sunk far faster than they could be replaced. Britain was down to a six-week supply of food.

Britain sought desperately for a way to stop the U-boats. It found one: the convoy, merchantmen sailing in groups protected by warships. Convoys had been used from the fourteenth century to the end of the Napoleonic Wars, but had been abandoned with the passing of the age of sail. History doesn't record who suggested resurrecting convoys in World War I, but it wasn't the British Navy. The Navy argued that convoys would require escort vessels better used

*A Navy recruiting poster from World War I promises extra pay
for each dive aboard a submarine.*

elsewhere, that the logistics were too complicated, and that convoys would simply attract more U-boats.

At the insistence of the French, ships carrying coal from Britain to France were put in convoys, and sinkings dropped from 25 percent to less than 1 percent. Atlantic convoys worked well, too; losses to U-boats were cut in half.

Before the introduction of convoys, U-boats would lie in wait for a ship to come along; now they had to go to the convoy, fire off a torpedo, dive deep, and try to escape. Submarine captain Karl Dönitz wrote in his memoirs, "The oceans at once became bare and empty; for long periods at a time the U-boats, operating individually, would see nothing at all." The heyday of the U-boat was over.

The early success of the German U-boats obscured the performance of the submarines of the other combatants.

Until Russia left the war, its nineteen submarines were divided between the Baltic, Arctic, and Black Seas. After Italy joined the Allies on May 24, 1915, its submarines operated in the Mediterranean. French submarines helped blockade the Dardanelles. Several Australian submarines supported the ill-fated landings at Gallipoli. American submarines made antisubmarine patrols in the Irish Sea and off the Azores, unglamorous but necessary duty. The number of submarines they sank was small compared to ship sinkings by U-boats, but still was substantial.

The terms of the armistice in 1918 stipulated that U-boats be surrendered in Allied ports. In a few months the vast U-boat fleet ceased to exist. During the war Germany had built some 360 submarines, and almost as many again were in construction at war's end. They sank more than

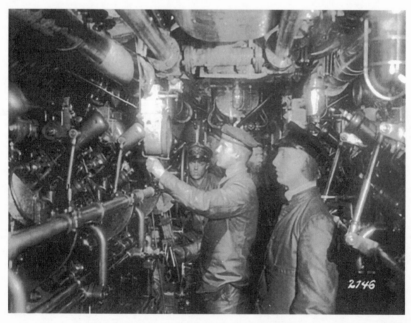

The engine room of an oil-burning German submarine, circa 1918.

eleven million tons of shipping and damaged nearly another eight million. The price was 178 U-boats sunk, 5,364 officers and crew dead—nearly 40 percent of those who served.

German submarines had come perilously close to turning the tide of the war, and the lesson wasn't lost on the major powers. They made submarine development a top priority in the years following the war. The Treaty of Versailles ruled that the Allies could use captured U-boats for research, and a number were distributed among the victors. The problem was that designers copied the wrong ideas. Germany had developed a large, clumsy cruiser submarine that proved of little use in the war. Despite this, America, Japan, Britain, France, and Italy all developed versions of the cruiser submarine.

Another idea that found favor was a submarine that could carry an airplane to scout for targets. In 1915 the *U-12* had launched a small floatplane off its foredeck. The American Navy in 1923 came up with a small seaplane that could be folded down to fit on a submarine. The British tried a variation, fitting a submarine with a catapult to shorten the time it took to launch a plane. Both countries abandoned their experiments, but the idea was taken up by the Japanese. They fitted a seaplane on their *Jun-Sun Type 1* cruiser submarine but, like the Americans, found that it took forever to get it launched, then, like the British, installed a catapult.

The French also caught cruiser-submarine fever. The 361-foot *Surcouf,* launched in 1934, carried a seaplane and was armed with two eight-inch guns. The designers claimed a surface range of 10,000 miles at ten knots.

Some countries, notably Italy and Japan, experimented with midget submarines, capable of taking a torpedo into range, firing it, and getting away.

The United States and Britain decided independently that smaller submarines were more practical. Japan built submarines of every size. Smaller countries were building coastal submarines. By 1931 there were 245 postwar submarines in the navies of twenty countries, including Peru, Finland, Portugal, Romania, Yugoslavia, and Chile.

At the 1921 Washington disarmament conference, the five major naval powers—Britain, the United States, France, Italy, and Japan—took up the problem of the submarine-building race. Britain tried to have the submarine banned. France opposed the measure, declaring that the submarine was the capital ship of the future. The United States and Japan also opposed banning submarines. The conference voted to permit Japan to increase the size of its Navy, a disastrous concession in light of later events.

The London Protocol of 1934 set down rules for the conduct of submarine warfare that echoed those of the Hague Convention of 1899: the submarine must surface before attacking; crews and passengers had to be guaranteed safety, and could not be abandoned in small boats on the high sea; merchant ships were not to be armed, or use their radios to call for help or to warn other ships at sea about submarines.

Many publicly denounced the rules as unrealistic. Among the dissenters were Winston Churchill, who would see Britain again nearly strangled by German submarines, and Karl Dönitz, who would show the world that submarines make their own rules.

Between the wars the U.S. Navy was plagued with submarine disasters. On March 25, 1924, the first U.S. submarine fatality occurred when the *F-4* failed to resurface after a dive off Honolulu. All hands were lost, but a salvage record was set when the boat was recovered from 306 feet. The recovery also set new records for deep-sea divers. Two officers, George Stillson and George French, in 1907 had developed techniques that enabled divers to descend to 274 feet. Divers on the *F-4* were able to work at 306 feet.

In September 1927 a liner unintentionally rammed and sank the *S-51* off Block Island, Rhode Island. Only three men escaped. Another submarine disaster occurred in December 1927 off Provincetown, Massachusetts, when the *S-4* plunged to the bottom. Bad weather forced rescuers to stop their attempts to reach the survivors, although they could hear tapping from the six men still alive in the forward torpedo room.

The Navy moved to improve submarine rescue operations. Two important devices were developed: the Momsen lung, a self-contained breathing apparatus that would allow submariners to escape to the surface, and the McCann Rescue Chamber, which could be lowered onto a stricken submarine. The chamber, adapted from a diving bell, would be locked into place over a special escape hatch built into the submarine's hull.

The chamber was put to good use after the new 310-foot SS-192, the *Squalus,* malfunctioned on a test dive off the New Hampshire coast on May 23, 1939, falling 243 feet to the ocean floor. Twenty-six men in the aft section were killed; the other thirty-three were trapped forward. While the world watched, a rescue fleet was hastily assembled and rushed to the scene. Lieutenant Commander Charles Momsen, designer of the Momsen lung, was in charge of all diving operations, including the first use of the rescue chamber. All the thirty-three men were rescued in four descents of the chamber. The *Squalus* was raised and refurbished, and served effectively in World War II.

The raising of the Squalus, *May 1939.*

In 1931 the British explorer Sir Hubert Wilkins and the Norwegian oceanographer Harold Sverdrup attempted to cross under the polar ice cap in a submarine. They obtained an obsolete fleet submarine from the U.S. Navy, renamed it the *Nautilus,* and with the help of designer Simon Lake added special equipment for the voyage—a pair of wooden runners mounted atop the superstructure. They planned to duck under the ice cap, increase positive buoyancy sufficiently to bring the runners in contact with the undersurface of the ice, then "ski" over it. There were enough gaps in the ice cap, they believed, to allow them to surface for air and to recharge the batteries.

There were flaws in their plan. Wilkins and Sverdrup tested the *Nautilus* under the ice and found that the runners scraping across the ice made a "quite terrifying" noise.

Breakdowns brought the crew to the brink of mutiny. Two crewmen sabotaged the diving planes, but Wilkins and Sverdrup pressed on until ice formed on the hull 500 miles from the North Pole. They gave up and went home.

Despite such ventures, submarines were considered first and foremost as instruments of war. In the mid-1920s the former Soviet Union asked German designers to help rebuild Russia's submarine fleet. By 1939 Russia would have 276 submarines.

Between the wars, Britain built a number of 191-foot U-class unarmed training submarines. When Hitler's designs on Europe became apparent, they were armed with six torpedoes. When war came, the British Navy also had nineteen fleet submarines in European waters, fifteen in the Far East, and fifteen Q-class boats assigned to training.

In the French Divisions des Sous-Marins were twenty-eight boats based at Toulon, seventeen at Bizerte, twelve at Casablanca, and a small squadron in the Pacific.

American submarine production was stepped up sharply when President Franklin D. Roosevelt signed the Naval Expansion Act. On the eve of World War II, the Navy had 103 submarines in service, 39 under construction, and another 43 in the planning stages.

The problem was that neither Britain, nor France, nor Russia, nor the United States knew the extent of the submarine construction program that had been going on for years in Nazi Germany.

6 | He's the Bravest Man I Know

Karl Dönitz was born into a family of Prussian aristocrats, and the Dönitz men either went into the military or became evangelical pastors. In a way, Karl Dönitz did both, except that his gospel was submarine warfare. A highly decorated U-boat captain in World War I, Dönitz was one of the few officers retained in what was left of the German Navy after the war.

In 1922 German engineers started a submarine company in Holland. Spain, Finland, Turkey, and several South American countries placed orders, and the first submarines were delivered in 1930. German naval officers and technicians taught the customers how to operate their new submarines. The firm was profitable, but its real purpose was to keep intact German submarine skills and technology.

Soon after Hitler became chancellor on January 30, 1933, the Navy quietly set up the Antisubmarine School at Kiel. It seemed innocent, defensive not offensive in intent, but it was the beginning of the rebirth of the German submarine service. Students wore civilian clothes, and went to the Finnish island of Abo in the summer to train on a Finnish submarine. At the same time, in violation of the Versailles Treaty, a closely guarded Kiel shipyard began building 250-ton submarines armed with three torpedo tubes and a deck gun. The school supplied the crews.

Hitler wrested military concessions from France and Britain in 1935, including permission to rebuild its Navy to 35 percent of the size of the British Navy. Three days after the treaty was signed, Hitler authorized building 24,000 tons of submarines. In six weeks, the first submarine from the Kiel shipyard went on patrol. Five more submarines entered service at two-week intervals.

Dönitz was the captain of the cruiser *Emden,* although he had been instrumental in setting up the submarine construction program. He studied the role that submarines might play if Germany and Britain tangled again. Just as Germany was developing submarine technology, Britain, he reasoned, would develop antisubmarine technology. He assumed that Britain would use convoys again, and he had an idea that he thought would be effective against convoys. He called it *Rudeltaktik,* later known as the "wolf pack." Submarines would work as a team; when one submarine found a convoy it would track it, calling in the others for a coordinated attack.

When the *Emden* returned from an Indian Ocean cruise in the summer of 1935, Admiral Erich Raeder, commander of the German Navy, met the ship and summoned Dönitz to command the submarine fleet, which now consisted of nine boats.

Dönitz tested his wolf pack tactics successfully in the 1937 naval war games in the Baltic Sea, convincing the admirals that wolf packs would be effective, given sufficient submarines. He wanted at least 300 submarines by the early 1940s, enabling 100 of them to be on patrol at all times.

Under Dönitz the submarine service was transformed into an elite force. Every man was a volunteer, and the training was long and hard, physically and mentally. Dönitz resisted attempts to politicize his submariners. Their loyalty was to the Fatherland and to him, not the Nazi party. He would pay a price for this, for the Nazis held the military purse strings.

At the North Sea port of Wilhelmshaven, Dönitz established a headquarters for his submarines and outfitted it

Germany's Krupp shipyard managed to build U-boats almost to the end of the war, despite intense Allied bombing.

with high-speed radio equipment to stay in constant communication with submarines at sea. He devised a chart system dividing the seas into fifty-square-mile grids on which to plot the location of submarines on patrol. If he knew where the submarines were and could communicate with them, he could call every shot.

His request for 300 submarines was pigeonholed. Hitler concentrated on rebuilding the Army. Naval funds were spent on capital ships. Hitler finally told Dönitz he would have his fleet—by 1948.

Hitler invaded Poland, and Britain and France declared war on September 3, 1939. Dönitz then had fifty-six submarines, only twenty-two of which were available for North Sea service. He cautioned his captains to follow the London Protocol rules: warships were fair game, but merchantmen, and most particularly passenger ships, were not to be sunk unless they were engaged in military activity.

It didn't take long for the rules to be broken. On the first afternoon of the war the *U-30*, commanded by Lieutenant Fritz-Julius Lemp, spotted the British liner *Athenia* off the coast of Ireland and sent it to the bottom with a torpedo. Lemp had disobeyed orders by not checking with Dönitz before attacking, and nearly was court-martialed.

The British also violated the rules. First Lord of the Admiralty Winston Churchill advised merchantmen to immediately radio for assistance on sighting a German submarine.

Two days after the sinking of the *Athenia,* the *U-48* ordered the steamer *Royal Sceptre* to stop. Instead, the ship speeded up and radioed for help. The *U-48* sent it to the bottom. In response, the admiralty began to arm merchantmen. The scene was being set for unrestricted submarine warfare.

In the harbor at Kiel, the new Nazi war flag is raised over the submarine fleet.

German submarines sank fifty-two ships in the first month of the war, including the aircraft carrier *Courageous.* They mined British ports, causing extensive damage to shipping. Destroyers sank the *U-39* when it attempted to close on the carrier *Ark Royal,* and sank another, the *U-27,* a few days later. But before the war was a month old, a German submarine shocked the Royal Navy.

Dönitz learned from one of his commanders that the guard ships weren't in place at Scapa Flow, the home base of the British Grand Fleet. Lieutenant Prien's *U-47* slipped undetected into Scapa Flow and torpedoed the *Royal Oak* as it lay at anchor. The battleship rolled over and sank, killing 823, including an admiral. In the confusion the *U-47* made it safely to the open sea.

In the aftermath of the sinking of the *Royal Oak,* Hitler personally presented Prien the Iron Cross, promoted Dönitz to rear admiral, and stepped up production of submarines. The chastened Royal Navy moved the fleet to the Atlantic side of Scotland until Scapa Flow's antisubmarine defenses were completed.

The first of Dönitz's wolf packs went into action in October 1939. It sank three ships the first day out, then found a convoy and, working in concert, sank three more. On the patrol, the wolf pack sank a total of eighteen ships.

Dönitz proposed building 56 500-ton submarines in 1940, 250 in 1941, and 348 in 1942. Hitler cut the plan drastically, not believing that wholesale sinking of Allied ships could bring victory.

In March 1940 Hitler invaded Norway and Denmark, ordering all available submarines to protect the invasion fleet. Torpedo problems limited their usefulness. Captains reported hitting British ships with torpedoes that didn't explode. Dönitz recalled the submarines from the Norwegian invasion to correct the torpedo problem, a decision that infuriated Hitler.

Crews waited in port while technicians sought to fix the torpedoes. After three months Dönitz sent a trusted captain, Viktor Ohrn, to sea in the *U-37* to test the corrected torpedoes. Ohrn sank 47,000 tons of shipping. The wolf packs were back in business.

In the spring of 1940 the Wehrmacht swept through Belgium and Holland and forced France out of the war. Now German submarines would no longer have to go through the North Sea and around Scotland to reach the Atlantic. Dönitz chose Lorient, southeast of Brest, as his new headquarters, with additional bases at Brest, La Pallice, Saint-Nazaire, and La Rochelle. Concrete, bombproof sub pens were built. Operating out of France extended the range of German submarines in the Atlantic 450 miles. In June they sank a record 260,000 tons of Allied shipping, nearly a ship a day. It was an amazing performance considering that only ten German submarines were at sea at a time.

The failure of Göring's Luftwaffe to win the battle of Britain was offset somewhat by the submarine campaign. Nazi propaganda sang the praises of the submarines. Captains were lionized, and their exploits thrilled Germany. Later in 1940 German submarines had two big kills in the Mediterranean—the carrier *Ark Royal* and the battleship *Barham*. Although Hitler didn't like Dönitz or his submarines, he finally was persuaded that they were crucial to victory.

A lethal variation of the wolf pack attack was devised by Otto Kretschmer, one of Dönitz's top captains. Instead of attacking frontally, he would submerge, slip under the escort vessels, surface within the convoy, torpedo everything in sight, submerge again and escape. On October 18, 1940, Kretschmer first used this tactic, sinking four ships. Another convoy soon lost seventeen ships to a wolf pack that slipped inside and fired torpedoes from the surface.

Wolf packs bedeviled convoys throughout 1941, and the Allied losses were staggering. Churchill, now prime minister, declared that the most vital part of Britain's struggle was to defeat the wolf packs. The British were having some success. Prien went down with the *U-37*, and Kretschmer was captured when a destroyer sank the *U-99*. But Germany was building submarines at a record rate, and new captains were setting new records. A captain automatically was awarded the Iron Cross after sending 100,000 tons of shipping to the bottom, oak leaves for the Iron Cross on reaching 200,000 tons. Seven captains earned oak leaves that year.

German submariners were shocked in August 1941 when a new captain surrendered the *U-570* to the British intact. No German officer in the prisoner-of-war camp would speak to him, and several plots were hatched to kill him. The British renamed the captured submarine the HMS *Graph* and used it to penetrate German waters.

When Hitler invaded Russia in 1941, Dönitz moved his submarines to attack shipping in the Baltic, but the pickings were slim. Not until big convoys began the Murmansk run would the hunting get better.

A stroke of luck changed the tenor of the war at sea. In May 1941 the *U-110* was abandoned while under attack off Greenland. The crew set timed explosives aboard to scuttle the submarine, but they failed to explode. A boarding party from a British destroyer discovered an Enigma code machine with a list of naval ciphers for the next month. Cryptographers cracked the German naval Hydra cipher. Now Britain knew where the German submarines were patrolling.

America was entering the battle of the North Atlantic. In September 1941 the destroyer USS *Greer* dropped depth charges on a German submarine and was nearly torpedoed in return. The U.S. destroyer *Reuben James* was sunk by a German submarine. Antiwar sentiment was running high in America, and Roosevelt did no more than express indignation.

Ambivalence about the war ended abruptly on the morning of December 7, 1941. Suddenly America was in a two-ocean war, ill prepared to fight either. Submarine defense was nearly nonexistent, and Churchill sent the chief of the Royal Navy's antisubmarine forces to Washington to give briefings. Construction was stepped up on destroyer escorts and escort carriers. But German submarines would make America pay for its unpreparedness.

Early in 1942 Germany broke the British and Allied merchant ship cipher. The Germans now knew the sailing

A German submarine in the rough seas of the North Atlantic, circa 1942.

dates, composition, and routes of convoys. Meanwhile, Dönitz shifted from the Hydra to a new Triton cipher, and the British couldn't crack it.

During 1942 U-boats sank more than six million tons of shipping. They cruised the eastern coast of the United States, sinking ships almost at will. Britain was close to being cut off from America. Dönitz believed that if monthly tonnage sunk increased from 650,000 to 800,000, the U.S. wouldn't be a factor in the European theater—whoever won the battle of the Atlantic would win the war.

Late in 1942 British cryptographers broke the Triton cipher and soon realized that the Germans were reading the Allies' convoy cipher. Before this could be turned to advantage, a new version of the German Enigma cipher machine was put in service.

Escort vessels and a new long-range patrol bomber, the B-24 Liberator, were coming into service by mid-1942, but what changed the complexion of the battle of the Atlantic was the Allied invasion of North Africa, called Operation Torch. Hitler ordered U-boats to the Mediterranean to harass Allied shipping there, reducing the effectiveness of the wolf packs in the Atlantic.

The fighting reached a new intensity in 1943. In March two wolf packs tried to trap convoy SC-121 in the North Atlantic. The battle lasted five days, and thirteen ships were sunk. The Germans cracked the new convoy code, and Dönitz sent forty submarines against two convoys steaming some 120 miles apart. The lead convoy of twenty-five ships was hit first; twelve ships were sunk in eight hours. In desperation the two convoys merged, but the submarines con-

"U-Boats Inside the Convoy," a painting by
English artist John Hamilton, depicts the German U-99
surfacing after torpedoing a British tanker.

tinued to attack, sinking a total of 140,000 tons before breaking off. The Allied escorts sank only one submarine.

Half a million tons were sunk in the first twenty days of
March. From July 1942 through March 1943 wolf packs sank
784 Allied ships. The convoy system was nearly discarded.

In 1943 Captain Daniel Gallery of the U.S. Navy managed to capture the *U-505*. The secret code books in the submarine's safe helped break the new version of Enigma. Now
the Allies knew where the German submarines were. In
April and May fifty-six submarines were sunk, another seventy-four in the following three months. Only fifty-eight
Allied ships were sunk in that period, a dramatic decrease.

Other factors also played a part in the turnaround.
Ships and planes employed in Operation Torch were returning to the Atlantic; advanced radar equipment made it easi-

The German U-boat U-505, *captured in 1943 and shown here flying the
American flag as it is towed into port. Codebooks in
the U-boat's safe unlocked the secrets of the new version of Enigma.*

er to detect submarines; the newness of the wolf pack operation had worn off; and inadequately trained crews were
manning the new German submarines.

Dönitz recalled his submarines in May for "regroup-
ing." Morale needed to be restored and new tactics developed before recommitting the submarines to the Atlantic.
Six weeks later Dönitz presented to Hitler the design for an
electro-submarine, a streamlined boat with a figure-8 hull
and a large battery capacity to give it more underwater
speed. A feature was automatic torpedo reloading—thirty
minutes were required to reload manually—which would
make the new submarine particularly deadly against convoys. Hitler ordered Albert Speer to have shipyards work
around the clock building the electro-submarine.

Another invention was the Walter turbine, which
burned a mixture of hydrogen peroxide and fuel oil and
would release sufficient oxygen to supply the submarine.
The turbine could propel a submarine underwater at speeds
in excess of twenty knots. Tests were encouraging, but the
turbine never saw service, partly because of its excessive fuel
consumption.

A device that saw service late in the war was the snorkel,
a breathing tube that permitted a submarine to stay below
the surface for indefinite periods. Late in the war, experimental submarines were equipped to fire the V-2 rocket
bombs.

But neither inventive genius nor courage regained the
German initiative in the Atlantic. At war's end, German sub-
marines were being systematically sent to the bottom. As
Russian troops entered Berlin, Hitler named Dönitz, now
Commander in Chief of the German Navy, to succeed him
as führer, then committed suicide.

Karl Doenitz, commander of the German Navy, at center after his capture at war's end. He is flanked by Albert Speer, left, and General Gustav Jodl, right.

On May 7, 1945, Dönitz radioed his captains to cease hostilities. Some refused to surrender and scuttled their boats. One sailed to South America to be interned, but most surrendered to the nearest warship to be escorted into port.

What had the German submarines accomplished? During the war they sank 175 warships and 2,828 merchantmen. Of the 1,162 submarines built, 784 were sunk. Some 32,000 of the 39,000 officers and men who served were killed.

At the outbreak of the war, Britain had fifty-eight submarines, most of them of modern design. They fought a type of war quite different from the U-boats, working in shallow waters strewn with mines and close to enemy bases with concentrations of antisubmarine forces. They were after warships, but few ventured out of port, and those that did were heavily escorted.

In the Mediterranean, British submarines operating out of Malta, Alexandria, and Gibraltar chopped away at Rommel's supply convoys, denying the Afrika Korps supplies during the battle of El Alamein. They also damaged the Italian Fleet sufficiently to make it useless for the rest of the war. In 1943 British submarines went to the Far East and scored well against Japanese shipping.

During the war British submarines sank 6 cruisers, 16 destroyers, 35 submarines, and 112 other warships, and damaged 2 battleships, 10 cruisers, 2 destroyers, 6 submarines, and 35 other warships. They also sank 493 merchantmen and damaged another 109. The cost: 75 British submarines sunk, some 35 percent of the 215 that served during the war; 3,416 submariners were killed, and 360 were taken prisoner.

Paying tribute to the submarine command at a postwar memorial service, Winston Churchill said, "Of all branches of men in the forces, there is none which shows more devotion and faces grimmer perils than the submariner. . . . Great deeds are done in the air and on land, nevertheless nothing surpasses your exploits."

Submarines in the Pacific

Submarines played a major role in the Pacific from the very beginning of the war. In Japan's attack on Pearl Harbor, its submarine force provided reconnaissance for the carrier strike force. However, midget submarines failed to gain entrance to Pearl Harbor, and four were sunk. Japan entered the war with some seventy-five submarines. During the war Japanese submarines primarily operated in conjunction with battle fleets.

The attack on Pearl Harbor nearly destroyed the American battle fleet in the Pacific. Practically all the U.S. Navy had to fight with were twenty-two submarines operating out of

Pearl Harbor and twenty-nine stationed at Subic Bay, near Manila. These were immediately deployed to attack the Japanese Fleet during the invasion of the Philippines, but their torpedoes let them down. Some were duds. Some ran so deep that even a zero depth setting sent them underneath their target. Others occasionally ran in a circle, striking the submarine that had fired them. The war would be half over before all the deficiencies were corrected. Only one Japanese ship was sunk during the Philippine invasion; the torpedo failure rate was nearly 100 percent.

Several submarine exploits in the Philippines captured the American imagination. The *Trout*, commanded by Lieutenant Commander F. W. Fenno, rescued several tons of gold belonging to the Bank of the Philippines from Corregidor before it could be captured by the Japanese. The

A Japanese midget submarine beached in Hawaii after the attack on Pearl Harbor, December 7, 1941.

Submarine base and oil tanks in Pearl Harbor in October 1941, just before the Japanese attack. None of these facilities was bombed—a fatal mistake for the Japanese.

Spearfish carried a boatload of nurses to safety, a feat dubbed Operation Petticoat.

Lieutenant Chester Smith became famous a few months later by taking his submarine into Tokyo Bay and sinking a heavily escorted 17,000-ton merchantman.

Intelligence gave the U.S. an advantage in the Pacific. In 1940 a team of cryptanalysts built a replica of the Japanese cipher machine, a breakthrough that led to the unraveling of Japanese naval and merchant marine ciphers. By the spring of 1942 the Navy could read parts of messages transmitted in the Japanese naval code. Combined with other intelligence, this gave a comprehensive and accurate picture of the battle plans for the attack on Midway.

Early in the morning of June 4, 1942, the submarine *Cuttlefish* sighted a Japanese tanker. Planes from Midway

Crews stand to quarters at a Japanese naval base, circa 1942.

investigated and discovered the tanker was part of a huge convoy. Nine submarines fanned out: the *Dolphin, Gato, Grayling, Grenadier, Grouper, Tambor, Trout, Nautilus,* and *Gudgeon.* Two other submarines—the *Cachalot* and the *Flying Fish*—approached the convoy from another direction.

The nine forward submarines attacked the Japanese fleet, and the battle of Midway was underway. The *Nautilus* sank the carrier *Soryu,* and the other submarines accounted for two cruisers, four destroyers, six Japanese submarines, and more than a hundred supply ships. The battle of Midway was an overwhelming victory for the U.S. Navy. Japan gambled heavily on taking Midway, but Admirals Chester Nimitz and Raymond Spruance, greatly outnumbered but armed with superb intelligence, broke the back of the Japanese invasion fleet.

Fleet Admiral Chester W. Nimitz, architect of the American victory at Midway, was a submarine officer early in his career.

In early 1943 crypt-analysts broke the cipher used to organize and direct convoys of Japan-ese merchantmen. Japan used a large merchant fleet to supply its troops scattered throughout the Pacific and to bring back essential goods: Japan imported 20 percent of its food, 24 percent of its coal, 88 percent of its iron ore, and 90 percent

A four-man gun crew loads and fires a deck gun from a submarine at a Japanese ship in the Pacific. Submarine captains liked to attack on the surface whenever possible, saving precious torpedoes.

At work on the hull of a submarine at the Electric Boat Company in Groton, Connecticut, August 1943.

of its oil. Like Britain, Japan was an island nation dependent on imports, but unlike Britain, Japan did not realize how vulnerable its lifeline was to a concentrated submarine attack. The Japanese Navy neglected antisubmarine warfare, and didn't develop radar until late in the war.

American submarines used wolf packs against Japanese shipping. Japanese convoys were small, so the wolf packs were usually three submarines. Commanders gave their submarines fanciful names—"Don's Devils," "Ben's Busters," "Laughlin's Loopers," "Ed's Eradicators"—and they roamed the Pacific savaging Japanese merchantmen. Theodore Roscoe wrote in *Submarine Operations in World War II,* "The atomic bomb was the funeral pyre of an enemy who had been drowned."

Submarine captains, particularly Lieutenant Commander Dudley Morton of the *Wahoo,* developed aggressive tactics to minimize the effect of a malfunctioning torpedo: the "down-the-throat" shot, for example, which involved firing a full salvo of six torpedoes at an attacking destroyer at point-blank range. Submarines often attacked on the surface at night. They used radar to choose a position for attacking, and evaded the escort ships with ease.

A factor in submarine performance in the Pacific was the leadership of Admiral Chester Nimitz, commander of the Pacific Fleet. As a young officer Nimitz had served on SS-2, the *Plunger,* and in World War I had commanded the American submarine force in the Atlantic. He loved submarines and knew how to mount a submarine campaign. From a few sinkings a month, his submarines increased their total to sixty-nine, more than two ships a day.

On the eve of the battle of Leyte Gulf in 1944, the *Darter* and the *Drum* bushwhacked a Japanese heavy cruiser squadron, sinking the *Atago* and the *Maya* and damaging the *Takeo.* In 1944 the *Albacore* torpedoed the new carrier *Taiho,* inflicting severe damage that led to its loss. Later the 62,000-ton battleship *Shinano* was torpedoed by the *Archerfish.*

Japanese submarines were much less effective. By going after warships, they exposed themselves to antisubmarine measures. One U.S. destroyer escort, the *England,* sank six Japanese submarines in twelve days. They got in some good punches, however. The carrier *Yorktown,* damaged during the battle of Midway, was under tow protected by four destroyers when the *I-168* found her. The submarine fired a salvo of four torpedoes, sinking both the carrier and the destroyer *Hasmann.* In 1942 the *I-19* torpedoed and sank the carrier *Wasp* south of the Solomons. A torpedo damaged the battleship *North Carolina.* Near the end of the war, the heavy cruiser *Indianapolis* was steaming unescorted between Guam and Leyte when it was sunk by the *I-58.* Of her crew of 1,196, 316 survived.

As their merchantmen were sunk, the Japanese relied on junks and coastal vessels to move supplies. These small boats could operate in waters too shallow for U.S. submarines. But by 1943 there were three flotillas of smaller British and Dutch submarines in the Far East, and they pressed the attack within the ten-fathom line. They also sank the cruisers *Kuma* and *Ashigora.*

A torpedoed Japanese ship goes down, seen through the periscope of an American submarine.

Japan used submarines to carry supplies to isolated garrisons. Special supply submarines, the I-361 class, had a surface range of 15,000 miles and could carry eighty-two tons of cargo. By 1945 most of Japan's fleet submarines were carrying supplies.

Japan built three 400-foot-long I-400-class submarines, the biggest in the world. They carried four floatplane bombers, and were meant to bomb the Panama Canal. None of them saw combat.

Japan had 2,337 merchantmen when the war began, 231 when it surrendered on August 14, 1945. Of the 190 submarines built for the Japanese Navy, 135 were sunk. Fifty-two American submarines were lost, about one of every four that served in the Pacific.

The nature of the American submarine campaign in the Pacific and the men who fought it can be found in the story of two submarines, the *Wahoo* and the *Tang*. According to Samuel Eliot Morison's epic, multivolume *History of United States Naval Operations in World War II*, the story began early in 1942 in Brisbane, Australia, where the *Wahoo* was being refitted. Her new captain was Dudley W. "Mush" Morton, and his executive officer was Richard Hetherington O'Kane.

Their first patrol was to Wewak, a harbor on the northeast coast of New Guinea that was being used as a Japanese staging area. The only map showing Wewak was in a school atlas. Morton enlarged a photograph of the map, traced the pertinent area on a nautical chart, and the *Wahoo* was underway.

Eight days later the *Wahoo* entered the harbor at Wewak and sighted a destroyer. Morton fired four torpedoes, but the destroyer evaded them all. Instead of crash-diving, Morton held his position as the destroyer closed at flank speed. When the range was 1,200 yards, Morton fired two torpedoes "down the throat" of the destroyer. The first missed, but the second hit dead center. The destroyer rose in the air and broke in two. The *Wahoo* made it out of the harbor through an artillery barrage.

Asked what it was like to look through a periscope and see a destroyer coming straight for him, Morton replied, "Don't ask me. I made O'Kane look. He's the bravest man I know." From the beginning Morton and O'Kane were a team; they thought alike and could exchange duties without missing a beat.

Three weeks after Wewak, the *Wahoo* found two Japanese freighters and sank them with three torpedoes. About to break off, Morton saw a troop ship, another freighter, and a tanker approaching. He sank the troop ship, crippled the freighter, then did an "end around" on the

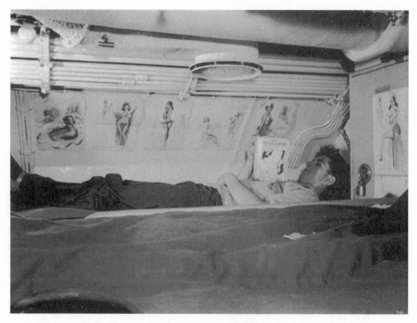

A submariner in his bunk aboard the USS Capelin, *1943.*

tanker, using the submarine's superior surface speed to slip ahead, submerge, and wait for it to come into range. The *Wahoo* crippled the tanker, but it continued to make headway. It was dark by now, but the hunt continued for the crippled ships. Morton caught up with the tanker and blew it apart with a brace of torpedoes.

Thirteen hours after first contact, he was getting the freighter in his sights when another destroyer steamed toward the scene. Morton did the unexpected, turning to head directly for the destroyer. The freighter headed for the destroyer, too, and when it closed Morton turned and sank it with his last two torpedoes. The submarine crash-dived and eluded the destroyer. When the *Wahoo* returned to Pearl Harbor, a broom was lashed to its periscope, the submariner's way of signaling a clean sweep.

The next patrol was to the Yellow Sea. In nineteen days the *Wahoo* sank nine ships, two sampans, and a trawler before running out of torpedoes. The broom went up again. The *Wahoo* was being overhauled when orders came through giving Dick O'Kane command of the newly commissioned *Tang*. When he left, it seemed in retrospect, he took the *Wahoo*'s luck with him.

Morton sailed the *Wahoo* to the Sea of Japan, the most dangerous area for an American submarine, and found it chock full of inviting targets, but every one of his torpedoes was faulty. He was seething when he reached Pearl Harbor. The admiral asked him what he wanted to do. "Load up with live fish this time and head back to the Sea of Japan," Morton replied.

His request was granted. But after a brief stop at Midway, the *Wahoo* made for the Sea of Japan, then simply disappeared. The Japanese said a submarine in the Sea of Japan sank four ships between September 29 and October 9, 1943, but the *Wahoo* was not listed among the American sub-

marines the Japanese claimed to have sunk during the war.

Dick O'Kane and the *Tang* made the Japanese pay for the *Wahoo*. Using the techniques Morton and he had developed, O'Kane and his crew of eighty-eight sank

An officer mans the periscope of an American submarine, 1942.

seventeen ships on their first patrol, thirty ships before they were through. But it was the fifth and last patrol that earned O'Kane and the *Tang* a place in history.

The *Tang* left Pearl Harbor September 24, 1944, bound for the Taiwan Strait, a seventy-five-mile-wide strip of water between China and Formosa. Japanese ships went through the strait bound for the Philippines, where the battle of Leyte was about to begin. Shortly after arriving the *Tang* sank two freighters.

O'Kane sighted a convoy of three tankers and two escorted troop ships. The *Tang* sped ahead of the convoy, positioning itself so that the ships would pass broadside. O'Kane was in the conning tower directing the firing. The tankers passed first and were blown apart. In the light of the burning ships, the lead transport saw the submarine on the surface and swerved to ram it. With no time to dive, the *Tang* lunged forward at hard-right rudder, sliding past the transport with inches to spare as gunfire sprayed the bridge of the submarine.

Once clear, the *Tang* fired its four aft torpedoes. Meanwhile, the transport, concentrating on ramming the submarine, had plowed into the other transport. The four torpedoes struck the two ships, both rose in the air in a series of explosions,

Commander Richard H. O'Kane
of the USS Tang.

fell back, and sank. The *Tang* had sunk the five-ship convoy in five minutes.

The next night the *Tang* found another convoy: two transports and a tanker guarded by two destroyers. O'Kane moved ahead and waited. When they came into range, he fired two torpedoes at each transport, and all four were hits. As the ships burned, two more Japanese ships appeared. As O'Kane prepared to attack, the destroyers started firing. The *Tang* managed to get off three stern torpedoes before the second destroyer arrived and prepared to ram the submarine.

The first torpedo hit a transport, the second hit the other transport, and the third caught the destroyer, blowing it out of the water. O'Kane, with only two torpedoes left, decided to finish off a crippled transport. He fired twice to make sure, then watched in horror as the final torpedo swung around and headed back like a boomerang toward the *Tang*.

The torpedo struck aft on the port side, and the sub started to sink quickly by the stern. The conning tower went under, and O'Kane and the eight others on the bridge struggled to free themselves. As they swam away, they could see their next-to-last torpedo blow up the crippled tanker. The bow of the *Tang* jutted up out of the water for a moment, then disappeared.

The survivors started swimming toward the shore but were picked up by a destroyer. The *Tang* was on the bottom under 180 feet of water, thirty of her crew still alive in the unflooded forward compartments. An electrical fire broke out in the battery room, forcing the men to seal themselves into the forward torpedo compartment. Deadly gas from the burning batteries seeped into the compartment, which was beginning to fill with water. The men put on Momsen lungs and started out the escape hatch. Thirteen got out; the others were overcome by the gas. More perished in the water. The Japanese rounded up the survivors.

Nine more died in a Japanese prison camp. Only O'Kane and five others lived to be repatriated at the end of the war. On his return home, Commander O'Kane was awarded the Medal of Honor for gallantry and bravery beyond the call of duty.

Despite the anonymous nature of submarine warfare, despite heroic deeds lost to posterity because they were performed on submarines that never returned, the submarine fleet in the Pacific for its size produced more heroes than any other branch of the Navy.

The Medal of Honor

In the war in the Pacific, seven submarine captains, including *Commander Richard Hetherington O'Kane,* whose exploits are recounted in this chapter, performed deeds of valor that earned them the Medal of Honor, America's highest military decoration.

Captain John Philip Cromwell, commander of a submarine attack group, was patrolling off the Japanese stronghold of Truk when the *Sculpin* was severely damaged by depth charges. He ordered the submarine to surface. Captain Cromwell was in possession of information concerning submarine strategy and tactics, fleet movements, and Admiral Nimitz's campaign. Rather than risk capture and the possibility of revealing secrets under Japanese torture, Captain Cromwell remained aboard as the damaged submarine plunged to the bottom.

On a moonlit night, a Japanese destroyer spotted the *Harder* on the surface and closed to attack. *Commander Samuel David Dealey* watched the destroyer come within

range, and sent it to the bottom with a torpedo. The submarine submerged, resurfaced, sank another destroyer,
then slipped into the nearby Japanese Tawi Tawi naval base,
where it sank two more patrolling destroyers. The *Harder*
escaped the open sea and the next day sighted an enemy
fleet. Commander Dealey torpedoed the lead destroyer,
then crash-dived. Five dangerous short-range torpedo
attacks had netted him five destroyers.

The *Barb* sank a large ammunition ship and damaged
other vessels during a patrol off China, then *Commander
Eugene Bennett Fluckey* spotted more than thirty enemy ships
in Mankwan Harbor. If he attacked, he would have to escape
by an hour's run at flank speed through uncharted, mined
waters. Slipping through the heavy enemy screen, he fired
the forward torpedoes at a range of 3,000 yards. Bringing
the stern tubes to bear, he fired four more torpedoes, scor-
ing a total of eight direct hits on six of the main targets. An
ammunition ship exploded, causing extensive damage to
nearby vessels. Commander Fluckey managed to clear the
area in the confusion. On the way home, he topped off an
epic patrol by sinking a Japanese freighter.

7 | *Underway on Nuclear Power*

In the early years of the Cold War, atomic energy and a human dynamo combined to produce the nuclear submarine, an event that would change the U.S. Navy as profoundly as the coming of steam. The human part of the equation was Hyman George Rickover, as unusual an officer as the Navy ever produced. He was short and slight, and looked frail. He commanded only one ship, a run-down minesweeper, and never saw combat. He rarely wore his uniform, and often publicly criticized Navy policy. The Navy had to be coerced by Congress into making him an admiral, and several times tried to force him to retire. He was fractious and unbending but a smooth politician. His mind could encompass the complexities of nuclear science and modern shipbuilding, and he had a vision: a nuclear navy.

Born the son of a tailor on August 24, 1898, at Makow, Poland, Rickover emigrated to America with his family and settled in Chicago. He was first in his class in high school, and shaved two years off his age to get into Annapolis.

As a young officer in the fleet, he was a loner, spending his free time tinkering in the engine room. After five years at sea, he returned to Annapolis and then went to Columbia University for advanced engineering training. He received a master's degree and a promotion to full lieutenant.

Rickover volunteered for submarine training and after graduation was assigned to the *S-48,* on which he spent three years. The next step would normally be command of a submarine, but there had been friction between Rickover and his superiors. He was sent instead to the Office of Inspector of Naval Materiel in Philadelphia and was put in charge of inspecting supplies and equipment. He continued his studies, writing an essay for the prestigious Naval Institute *Proceedings* on "International Law and the Submarine," which concluded:

> The submarine is the weapon par excellence of the weak naval power. Control of the seas can never be obtained through possession of a submarine fleet, no matter how large. But control of the seas can be effectively challenged and its exercise rendered hazardous by submarine operations.

Rickover became assistant engineering officer of the battleship *New Mexico,* helped his department win three Navy "E"s for efficiency, and earned a reputation as a fanatic. One officer recalled, "He had special plugs made and inserted in the showerheads, cutting the water down to a trickle. And then he started timing junior officers' showers. If he thought you were taking too long, he'd pull you out of the shower."

Admiral Hyman G. Rickover,
"father of the nuclear navy,"
on the deck of a submarine
headed out to sea.

Rickover then com-
manded a wooden mine-
sweeper on river patrol in
China for a few months.
It was the only ship he
would ever command.

A few years later
Rickover was sent to the
Bureau of Engineering,
where he worked with officers as talented as himself. When
war came he was made chief of the electrical section of the
Bureau of Ships. He redesigned a number of parts and
forced the manufacturers into making the changes.

In 1944 the huge Navy supply depot in Mechanicsburg,
Pennsylvania, was mired in red tape and inefficiency.
Rickover, now a captain, fired a number of supervisors and
shaped up the survivors. Soon supplies moved to the fleet 25
percent faster. On Okinawa in 1945 he expanded the fleet
repair facilities. His commanding officer said, "A more con-
scientious man never lived."

After the war, Rickover took charge of mothballing
ships on the West Coast. He now could retire and use his
executive talents in civilian life. But he wasn't through with
the Navy yet.

In Oak Ridge, Tennessee, a joint military-civilian task
force was finding practical uses for atomic energy. Rickover
headed the Navy team. The Navy, one of the greatest users
of power in the world, thought atomic energy could be

used for ship propulsion. Rickover quickly grasped the technology of atomic power and foresaw how it could transform the Navy.

Control of atomic energy was being transferred from the military Manhattan Project to the new civilian Atomic Energy Commission. General Kenneth Nichols, head of the Manhattan Project, asked Rickover to prepare a Navy position paper. Hospitalized while awaiting a hernia operation, Rickover summoned his assistant, borrowed secretaries from the hospital, and wrote the paper in two days. It stated that the Navy could have a nuclear-powered submarine within the next five to eight years. The Navy said that was overly optimistic.

Rickover became a crusader, ignoring the chain of command to push his ideas to admirals, scientists, congressmen—anyone with influence who would listen. The Navy disbanded his team; he simply worked harder. The first breakthrough came with the Oak Ridge scientists, who started working in their spare time in support of his nuclear submarine. But he still had to convince the Navy.

He spent two months composing a letter to Admiral Chester Nimitz, chief of naval operations. He stressed the practical importance of a nuclear submarine, and how the Bureau of Ships and the AEC could work together to build it. Nimitz and the secretary of the Navy both approved Rickover's proposal, only to have it vetoed by the AEC. Rickover was given command of a new nuclear department at the Bureau of Ships.

In 1949 the AEC reversed its veto and created a Naval Reactors Branch under Captain Rickover. The prestige of the Navy was now on Rickover's shoulders.

Rickover pressured Westinghouse to develop a nuclear power plant small enough to fit into a submarine. By insisting that modifications to the prototype immediately be incorporated into a second plant, he cut months off the development time. The Electric Boat Company would build the first nuclear submarine, to be named the *Nautilus.*

Rickover now was a man possessed, as if he himself were powered by atomic energy. He drove everyone around him unmercifully. Nothing less than perfection was tolerated. Engineers could not get a single modification of specifications. Suppliers who did not come up with the exact items did them over or lost the contract.

Fifty-foot models of the *Nautilus* were built and blown up by miniature depth charges to test for weakness. On learning the Navy was using old submarines to test depth charges, Rickover had vital parts of the *Nautilus* put aboard. When they failed to stand up to the blasts, he blistered the suppliers for "selling him junk." The parts improved substantially. He saw himself at war, with "mediocrity, bureaucracy, and inefficiency."

Rickover was passed over for rear admiral in 1951. The next year the public became aware of the *Nautilus* project and Rickover. He was awarded the Legion of Merit "for meritorious conduct in the performance of outstanding services to the government. . . ." The next day he again was passed over for rear admiral. An officer passed over twice was expected to resign within six months.

A campaign was mounted to save Rickover. Senator Henry Jackson and Representative Sidney Yates spoke up for Rickover, and the media gave the controversy wide play. The pressure mounted, and in 1953 Rickover was made a rear admiral.

On January 21, 1954, within the eight years Rickover had promised, Mamie Eisenhower swung a bottle of champagne to launch the sixty-five-million-dollar *Nautilus.* The 320-foot

Launching ceremony for the Nautilus, *the world's first nuclear-powered submarine (1954).*

craft could travel underwater for more than 100,000 miles on the power of a nuclear mass the size of a baseball. The sea trials were a vindication for nuclear propulsion. The book *Rickover: Controversy and Genius* by Norman Polmar and Thomas B. Allen quotes an Electric Boat report:

> In many ways, *Nautilus* can be considered the first real submarine. Previously, submarines had really been surface vessels capable of submerging for short periods at best. *Nautilus* is the first ship whose natural habitat is the depths themselves.

Admiral Rickover saw what a nuclear submarine would mean to the Navy. "The *Nautilus* is not merely an improved submarine, she is the most potent and deadly weapon afloat. She is, in fact, a new weapon. Her impact on naval tactics and strategy may well approach that of the airplane."

Except for its atomic reactor, the *Nautilus* was a larger version of the conventionally powered Tang-class submarine, with six torpedo tubes and a large passive sonar in the bow. And the *Nautilus* had a major problem: its cooling pumps could be heard ten miles away. A second atomic submarine, the *Seawolf,* was launched early in 1957, followed shortly by the *Skate.* Beginning with the *Nautilus,* atomic submarines would be called ships, not boats; they now had the size and power of surface ships.

The *Nautilus* set new standards for underwater performance. On one 265-hour underwater voyage, it averaged 19.1 knots, unbelievable by conventional submarine standards. Its finest hour came in the summer of 1958 in a top secret mission called Operation Sunshine. The *Nautilus* was ordered to sail from Honolulu to Portland, England, passing under the Arctic ice cap. At the same time, the captain of the *Skate,* Commander James F. Calvert, was ordered to sail to the Arctic to "develop techniques for surfacing in ice packs."

The *Nautilus* passed under the North Pole on August 3, 1958, surfacing beyond the ice cap five days later. Captain William Anderson radioed the historic message: *"Nautilus*

Commander William Anderson of the Nautilus, *sender of the historic message* "Nautilus *ninety north" from under the polar ice cap.*

ninety north." It was under the polar ice for ninety-five hours, traveling 1,830 miles. The voyage was perilous. The waters under the ice cap were uncharted, and the *Nautilus* was virtually blind, except for sonar and a television camera to look up at the ice. A hull puncture or damage to its propellers would have doomed the submarine and the crew.

The *Skate* passed under the North Pole nine days after the *Nautilus*. Near the pole it surfaced in a polynya, a sheet-ice skylight, using its great weight to break through the ice. The *Skate* broke through the ice eight more times on the voyage. In 1962 the *Skate* surfaced at the pole itself. Other polar voyages tested a new inertial navigation system.

"Characteristics of Certain Submarines"

In his report, "The Characteristics of Certain Submarines," Commander Louis Roddis, an assistant to Admiral Rickover, presented these comparisons of the two *Nautilus* submarines to the Society of Naval Architects and Marine Engineers.

Date	1874	1954
Name	*Nautilus*	*Nautilus*
Length	232 feet	320 feet
Beam	26 feet	27½ feet
Surface displacement	1,417.6 tons	3,530 tons
Submerged displacement	1,507 tons	4,040 tons
Hull construction	double hull	double hull
Hull thickness	2½ inches	(not given)
Propulsive power	single; 20-foot diameter	twin screw
Propulsion plant	electric	geared steam turbine
Maximum speed	50 knots	"over 20 knots"
Cruising range	43,000 miles	62,562 on first core; 91,324 on second; 150,000 on third
Building yard	a desert island	Electric Boat Co.
Cost	£147,500	$65 million
Armament	ram	6 torpedo tubes; some 20 torpedoes
Owner	Prince Dakarr of India	U.S. government
Captain	Captain Nemo	Commander E. P. Wilkinson
Collapse depth	4,800 feet	over 600 feet

New hydrodynamic theories were incorporated in the *Albacore,* an unconventional-looking submarine with a whale-shaped hull, a streamlined sail, and two propellers contrarotating on a single shaft. Inspired by aerodynamic research on blimps and dirigibles, the hull provided significantly higher maneuverability and speed.

The lessons of the *Albacore* were incorporated into the largest and most powerful submarine of its time, the $109-million USS *Triton.* At 447.5 feet the hull was longer than two average city blocks, and its nuclear reactors produced as much horsepower as the engines of a light cruiser. The *Triton* was launched August 19, 1958. As sea trials were ending, its captain, Edward Beach, was summoned to the Pentagon and asked, "Beach, you're about to start your shakedown cruise. Can *Triton* go around the world—submerged—instead?"

On February 16, 1960, the *Triton* secretly sailed off on the route taken by Magellan in 1519. From Spain, it steamed south in the Atlantic, rounded Cape Horn into the Pacific, across Magellan Bay in the Philippines, then south through Lombok Strait in Indonesia, through the Indian Ocean, around the Cape of Good Hope, up to the coast of Spain, then across the Atlantic to the United States. The submarine surfaced off Delaware on May 10, 36,000 miles and eighty-three days and ten hours after its departure. The *Triton* surfaced briefly twice on the voyage, once to transfer a sick seaman, and off the coast of Spain to honor the country from which Magellan had sailed.

A helicopter took Captain Beach off the *Triton* and flew him to the south lawn of the White House. President Eisenhower presented Beach with the Legion of Merit, and awarded the *Triton* the Presidential Unit Citation. At the president's side during the ceremony was Admiral Rickover.

The voyage of the *Triton* had political considerations. It was timed to bolster American prestige at a summit meeting with Soviet leader Nikita Khrushchev. But just before the end of the record voyage, Russia shot down Francis Gary Powers's U-2 spy plane. Eisenhower refused to apologize for the U-2 incident, and Khrushchev walked out of the Paris summit.

By the end of 1960 the Navy had thirteen nuclear submarines in service and another thirty-five under construction or authorized for construction. Three nuclear surface ships were being completed, and they would form an all-nuclear task force: the supercarrier *Enterprise* and the missile cruisers *Bainbridge* and *Long Beach.*

Admiral Rickover now supervised all the Navy's nuclear propulsion systems and, more important, virtually controlled all key personnel on nuclear vessels. He personally interviewed, selected, and supervised the training of submarine officers, many of the senior enlisted men, and the captains and engineering officers of the surface ships.

To be part of the Naval Reactors Branch required a personal interview with Rickover. The interviews were legendary, involving harassment, verbal abuse, and demeaning indignities. Critics said Rickover's concern was with the reactor itself, not with the qualities that made great submarine commanders. Jimmy Carter recalled his interview with Rickover in his book *Why Not the Best?*

> I had applied for the nuclear submarine program, and Admiral Rickover was interviewing me for the job. It was the first time I met Admiral Rickover and we sat in a large room by ourselves for more than two hours, and he let me choose any subjects I wished to discuss. Very carefully, I chose those about which I knew most at the time—current events, seamanship, music, literature, naval tactics, electronics, gun-

nery—and he began to ask me a series of questions of
increasing difficulty. In each instance, he soon proved that I
knew relatively little about the subject I had chosen.

He always looked right into my eyes, and he never smiled.
I was saturated with cold sweat.

In selecting candidates, Rickover often passed over Annapolis graduates for NROTC cadets who had majored in
engineering, physics, or mathematics at leading schools.
The program was designed to make engineers out of
physicists, and physicists out of engineers. Rickover was
leery of links to the "real" Navy. One candidate was rejected
simply because his father was an admiral. There was no
court of appeal; Rickover's decisions were final. Beyond
talent and energy, Rickover sought total loyalty.

Rickover appeared so often before congressional com-
mittees that he was known as "the Admiral of the Hill." From
the late 1940s to the early 1980s he positioned himself as the
Navy's only true believer in nuclear power. A typical
Rickover statement came in testimony before the House
Armed Services Committee on April 18, 1967: "We have got
somehow to drag the Navy into the twentieth century. From
the beginning the Navy has opposed nuclear power. Were it
not for this committee, the Joint Committee on Atomic
Energy, and the Senate Armed Services Committee, we
would not have nuclear submarines."

No evidence supports the charge that the Navy
opposed nuclear power. There is ample evidence, though,
that the Navy opposed Rickover and his personal freedom.
But Rickover apparently considered anyone who opposed
him, what he did, or how he did it to be an opponent of a
nuclear navy.

The Navy was eager to join the underwater capabilities
of the nuclear submarine with the destructive power of the

intercontinental ballistic missile (ICBM). In the 1950s the U.S. worried about the possibility of a preemptive Soviet missile strike against its land-based ICBMs. But missiles on submerged submarines would be immune from attack, ready to launch a second strike.

No place on earth is more than 1,700 miles from the sea, within reach of submarine-launched intermediate-range missiles (IRBMs). The trick was to keep a submarine on station months on end, fixing its position precisely enough for missile accuracy. With the technology of the time, to get a precise fix a submarine had to surface, which could betray its position.

In 1956 work began on a system, named Polaris, to launch IRBMs from submarines. Scientists speculated it might take twenty years. In the wake of Sputnik, President Kennedy stepped up the program, and on July 20, 1960, the *George Washington* submerged off Cape Canaveral, Florida, and fired two A-1 Polaris missiles at a target 1,200 miles away. The report flashed back: "From out of the deep to target. Perfect."

Within the year the second fleet ballistic-missile submarine (SSBN), the *Robert E. Lee,* stayed submerged sixty-six days to set a new record.

Polaris made the *Nautilus* obsolete. Unsuited for conversion to missiles, it was decommissioned in May 1980.

Two technical innovations made the Polaris system work. The SINS (ship inertial navigation system) computed the submarine's course accurately, without reference to either magnetic or true north. SINS uses accelerometers and gyroscopes to plot all drift and movement in relation to a known point. Accuracy improves with additional fixes, but even one initial fix is adequate to provide coordinates for the missile fire control computer.

The second innovation was the development of an oxygen generator and "scrubbers" to filter and clean the air inside a submarine, allowing it to be rebreathed. With scrubbers a submarine could stay submerged on station for months at a time.

Polaris was the deadliest weapon system of its time. One submarine carrying sixteen missiles equipped with hydrogen warheads could deliver more explosive power than all the bombs dropped in World War II. The ballistic submarine is a doomsday machine.

In 1979 President Carter said, "As an ex-submariner, one who was in the initial program, I am personally biased. But I think that if there ever has been any one single weapon system that has ensured our nation's integrity and security, it has been the nuclear submarines with a strategic weapon capacity."

The system has been constantly improved. The A-1 Polaris missile was replaced in 1966 by the A-3, increasing the effective range to 2,880 miles. In 1970 a new missile was introduced: the C-3 Poseidon with three multiple independent reentry vehicle (MIRV) warheads. Each warhead proceeds to its own target, creating a shotgun effect to confuse ABM (antiballistic missile) defenses.

The nuclear submarine program has suffered setbacks. On April 10, 1963, the *Thresher,* the first of a new class of attack submarines, failed to surface from a deep dive 220 miles off Boston and was lost with its 129-man crew. In May 1968 the *Scorpion* and its crew of ninety-nine were lost 400 miles southwest of the Azores.

Rickover once told a congressional committee, "If you want to have real responsibility you must make a competent man responsible for the entire project and not let him say, 'Well, I'm here two years and if something goes wrong it was

The USS Thresher, *lost in 1963 with 129 men aboard in the Navy's worst peacetime submarine disaster.*

the fault of my predecessor.' I can never say that. . . . If anything goes wrong, I'm responsible." However, on the night the *Thresher* went down, Rickover called the chief of the Bureau of Ships to make it clear that he, Rickover, was not responsible for the *Thresher.*

The rapid development of Polaris gave the United States a strong advantage over the Soviet Union, and the Red Navy moved to close the gap. The first Soviet missile-carrying submarines, the Juliett and Echo classes, were no match for Polaris. But improvements came quickly after 1960. The diesel-powered Golf class carried the SS-N-5 Serb missile with a 650-mile range and could launch it underwater. The first Soviet nuclear-powered submarines were the 3,700-ton Hotel class, armed similarly to the Golfs. Between 1967 and 1971 the Soviets launched thirty-three Yankee-class submarines, comparable to the American SSBNs. Each carries sixteen SS-N-6 Sawfly missiles, with an estimated range of 1,300 miles.

The first Royal Navy nuclear submarine was the HMS *Resolution* in 1967, and it was a curious hybrid: the hulls were British; the missiles, tubes, and fire control technology, American. When the *Resolution* was commissioned, a wag posted a sign on the missile compartment that read, "You are now entering the American Zone."

France had planned to use Polaris technology, but poor relations with the de Gaulle government prompted the United States to veto the idea. An equivalent program was launched, the Mer-Sol-Ballistique-Strategique (MSBS) M-2. Five French nuclear submarines were built in the 1970s, and now comprise the Sousmarins Nucleaire Lance Engins (SNLE), operating in the Atlantic out of Brest.

Rickover, almost forced to retire in 1952, rose to the rank of full admiral and stayed on active service until 1982, fifty-nine years after his Annapolis graduation. No U.S. Navy officer ever served longer.

8 | An Infinitesimal Atom Floating in Illimitable Space

The natural habitat of a submarine is the ocean depths, but until recently the ocean depths were almost as incomprehensible as the dark side of the moon. Man sailed around the world long before he knew how deep was the ocean, let alone what went on down there. Ferdinand Magellan, the Portuguese circumnavigator, attempted to measure the depth of the water at a point between the islands of Saint Paul and Tiburon in the South Pacific. His device failed to touch bottom, so he concluded that his ship was over the deepest part of the ocean.

A submarine theorist, Father Georges Fournier, wrote in 1647 that the greatest depth of the ocean "was about 400 fathoms," some 2,400 feet. Not till 1962 did a British survey determine that the ocean reached a depth of 37,782 feet in the Challenger Deep in the Mariana Trench, 200 miles southeast of Guam.

Ponce de León didn't find the Fountain of Youth, but in 1513 he reported the existence of the Gulf Stream, the giant river in the sea that originates in the Gulf of Mexico, passes through the Straits of Florida, then travels north along the coast of the United States before crossing the Atlantic.

Benjamin Franklin was an early student of the effects of the Gulf Stream. He noted, for example, that ships from the colonies reached England sooner than ships from England reached America. His interests included sea temperatures and sea life. Franklin is considered by some to be the father of oceanography.

In 1794 President George Washington appointed Captain Thomas Truxton the first Oceanographer of the United States. Oceanography then was defined as the study of all the sciences having any relationship to the sea: geology, astronomy, physics, chemistry, marine biology, among others. Captain Truxton was one of the first to use water temperature as a means of determining location at sea.

In 1804 Nathaniel Bowditch, a mathematician, published *The New American Practical Navigator,* which still is a standard work. The first Navy hydrographic chart was produced in 1811 when the USS *Constitution* surveyed New London harbor. Charles Wilkes, a naval officer, was in charge of a scientific expedition that sailed around the world from 1838 to 1843 collecting data. He wrote books filled with information on deep soundings, subsurface currents, underwater temperatures, marine biology, tides, and the characteristics of waves.

In the 1840s Matthew Fontaine Maury, head of the Navy Depot of Charts and Instruments, devised a system of extracting oceanographic information from ships' logs to supplement the findings of scientific expeditions. As a result of his studies, sea captains were able to cut an average of 48 days off the 183-day voyage from New York around Cape Horn to San Francisco. Congress was sufficiently impressed with this to give Maury three ships for further oceanographic research.

In 1850 Maury's *The Physical Geography of the Sea* demolished the popularly held belief that the seabed was flat. "Could the waters of the Atlantic be drawn off," Maury wrote, "so as to expose to view this great sea gash, which separates continents, and extends from the Arctic to the Antarctic, it would present a scene most rugged, grand and imposing. The very ribs of the solid earth would be brought to life."

Maury pointed the way to modern echo sounders, or depth gauges, by suggesting that a bomb be exploded or a bell rung and the echo from the bottom be timed and recorded. A young associate of Maury, Midshipman John Mercer Brook, perfected a workable deep-sea sounding device to sample the bottom of the ocean.

Commodore Matthew Perry's expedition to Japan in the early 1850s produced a wealth of geographical surveying in Far East waters. Lieutenant Silas Bent made the first extensive study of the Kuroshio Current. Maury, while involved in surveying the seabed between Ireland and Newfoundland preparatory to laying the first transatlantic telegraph cable, learned that, contrary to scientific theory, marine life did exist below 300 fathoms.

From 1872 through the turn of the century, oceanographic expeditions were launched by many countries. The British ship *Challenger* made important findings. German ships explored the South Atlantic and Indian Oceans. A

Dutch expedition worked around the Indian archipelago; a Scandinavian expedition surveyed the Arctic Ocean and its approaches. The Germans and Belgians were active in the Antarctic. The USS *Enterprise* sailed around the world collecting samples of the seabed. And two useful publications were issued by the U.S. Navy Hydrographic Office: the first magnetic chart of the world in 1882, followed the next year by *Pilot Charts* containing valuable wind and current information.

The tide of oceanographic information was slowed by the Spanish-American War and World War I, but picked up again in the 1920s. Dr. Harvey C. Hayes, a scientist employed by the U.S. Navy, developed the sonic depth finder in 1921, and three years later the Hydrographic Office published its first bathymetric chart based on sonic soundings. The German ship *Meteor* made thirteen crossings of the South Atlantic from 1925 to 1927, taking some 40,000 soundings. The expedition yielded up valuable information on the circulation of seawater, wave movements and force, and sedimentary deposits.

Oceanographic institutions came into being in the 1920s: the University of Oslo's biological station, the Oceanographic Museum at Monaco, the Geophysical Institute at Bergen, and the Woods Hole Oceanographic Institution in Massachusetts.

The first oceanographer to capture the imagination of the public was Dr. William Beebe, a naturalist and the director of tropical research of the New York Zoological Society. He explored South America, Borneo, and the Himalayas before turning to the world beneath the sea.

Beebe was working on a design for a diving bell when he met Otis Barton, a young geologist-engineer with ideas of his own. They teamed up to build a diving bell, 4 feet 9 inch-

*Dr. William Beebe, left, and Otis Barton with the bathysphere in
which they descended to a record 3,036 feet in 1934.*

es in diameter with 1½-inch-thick walls, weighing 5,000
pounds. The air supply was contained in the bell, two cylinders of oxygen and chemicals for removing carbon dioxide,
but the bell relied on a tender for electricity. Beebe called
the bell a "bathysphere," from the Greek for "deep sphere."

The inspiration for the bathysphere probably came
from an Italian count, Piatti Del Pozzi, who in 1897 designed
and built a spherical submersible named *La France.* The
walls of his bell were three-inch iron to withstand the pressure at great depths. The bell, equipped with portholes and
an electric floodlight, was lowered from a barge, and working arms enabled Count Del Pozzi to handle tools while
working on sunken ships.

Beebe's bathysphere was built to go deep. In its first
unmanned test off Bermuda in 1930, it was lowered to 1,500

feet. Then Beebe and Barton took her down. Beebe was fascinated by the blue world he saw outside the bell. "It excited our optic nerves in a most confusing manner," he said. "We kept thinking and calling it brilliant. . . . I brought all my logic to bear, I put out of mind the excitement of our position in watery space and tried to think sanely of comparative color, and I failed utterly." They descended to 800 feet, well beyond the limit of visibility, before returning to the surface.

A floodlight was rigged outside the bell, and Beebe decided to take the bathysphere to its ultimate safe depth, 1,428 feet. Beebe used a spectroscope while descending to study the gradual disappearance of colors from the surrounding water. Red was the first to go at 20 feet, followed by orange at 150 feet; by 350 feet the yellow was almost gone; at 450 feet no blue remained, just violet and a hint of green; then at 800 feet only a pale gray. Outside the porthole the water was almost black.

Beebe turned on the searchlight to make notes on the marine life he found. At some levels there was nothing to see. At other levels the sea was alive with fish. The bell stopped at 1,400 feet, the water pressure now at slightly more than 650 pounds per square inch. Beebe said he looked down "into the black pit-mouth of hell itself." Quoting philosopher Herbert Spencer, he said he felt as if he were "an infinitesimal atom floating in illimitable space."

Beebe and Barton made improvements in the bathysphere and returned to Bermuda in 1932 for additional experiments, reaching a depth of 2,175 feet. They descended to 3,036 feet two years later, and continued diving at depths from 500 to 3,000 feet until the onset of World War II. No further records were set, but their purpose was not to set new diving records but to develop the technology for the bathysphere. They compiled a remarkable record of marine life at depths never before reached.

A Swiss physics professor followed Beebe's dives with interest. A month before Beebe's 2,200-foot dive, the professor, Auguste Piccard, ascended to a record of 55,557 feet in a balloon. Piccard noted that the bathysphere was dangerously vulnerable because it was lowered and raised by a single steel cable. He thought the bathysphere should be independent with its own buoyancy system.

By the late 1930s Piccard found the money to put his ideas into practice. The Belgian government financed his "bathyscaph," Greek for "deep boat," but construction was interrupted by the war. When completed, the bathyscaph was a sphere seven feet in diameter suspended below a sixty-five-foot cylindrical float, which acted as the buoyancy chamber. The bathyscaph's hull was designed to withstand water pressure at a depth of 13,000 feet.

The French Navy's underwater research group sent observers to the bathyscaph's sea trials, including Jacques-Yves Cousteau. The thin-walled float, damaged in a preliminary dive, was judged too fragile, and the tests were called off. Piccard was in danger of losing his backing, but

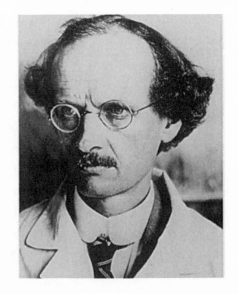

Deep-diving pioneer Auguste Piccard, who took his bathyscaph down to 10,395 feet in 1953.

Cousteau worked out an agreement between Belgium and France to build a new bathyscaph with Piccard serving as a consultant.

Piccard had differences with the French and dropped out. He raised enough money for a new bathyscaph, the *Trieste,* and in August 1953 he and his son Jacques took it down 10,395 feet off Italy. Feeling vindicated, Piccard turned the project over to his son and returned to teaching. The *Trieste* had several improvements, including a forged hull allowing deeper dives, and a stronger, more stream-lined buoyancy tank.

The French tested their bathyscaph off Dakar, Senegal, on February 15, 1954, taking it to a record 13,282 feet. The government authorized a larger, more sophisticated bathy-scaph, to be called the *Archimede,* to dive in the unexplored Challenger Deep, where depths approached seven miles.

Jacques Piccard attracted the attention of Dr. Robert Dietz of the U.S. Office of Naval Research, who thought the *Trieste* might open up new areas of oceanographic research. The Navy bought the *Trieste* in 1957, beefed it up, and set out to beat the French to the bottom of the Challenger Deep. In January 1960 Jacques Piccard and Lieutenant Don Walsh, a submarine officer, took the *Trieste* down to 30,000 feet at a rate of 3 feet a second, then slowed to 1 foot a second to ensure a soft landing. They touched down at a depth of 35,800 feet, startled to see fish outside the porthole where the pressure exceeded seven tons per square inch. They sur-faced safely, four minutes ahead of schedule. President Eisenhower presented Piccard the Navy's Distinguished Public Service Award and Walsh the Legion of Merit.

The *Trieste* was called into service when the nuclear sub-marine *Thresher* sank in 1963 off the coast of Massachusetts. It located the wreckage of the submarine scattered across the ocean floor 8,400 feet down. The submarine apparently had imploded.

The Navy built a bigger, better *Trieste II* in 1963, but Piccard returned to Switzerland to work with his father on a "mesocaph," a diving boat designed to work at middle depths. Failing to find sufficient financing, Jacques proposed that the mesocaph be built to take visitors to the international exhibition at Lausanne on an underwater cruise of Lake Geneva. The idea was accepted, the funding provided, and the *Auguste Piccard* became Switzerland's first and only submarine. It accommodated forty passengers, each seated in a swivel chair with a personal porthole. Floodlights illuminated the water outside, and closed-circuit television showed the passengers how the submarine looked from without. The vessel made 13,000 dives in more than 300 feet of water without mishap.

Piccard was retained to propose projects for Grumman Ocean Systems, and he gave them an ambitious one—exploration of the Gulf Stream. NASA joined in to study what effect virtual isolation for a long period would have on the crew. Another participant in the Gulf Stream project, the Naval Oceanographic Office, wanted to study the deep scattering layer, a strange phenomenon of great importance to submarine detection that occurs when sonic and ultrasonic waves are bounced from the surface to the ocean floor and back. At different depths, layers of unknown origin sometimes appear in the water and reflect the electronic waves, creating the effect of a false bottom under which an enemy submarine could lie undetected. The layers rise at night and sink during the day, often as much as 4,000 feet. If the PX-15 could solve the mystery of this deep scattering layer, the Navy might be able to make improvements in antisubmarine warfare.

The PX-15 was completed early in 1968 at a cost of $2.5 million and named the *Ben Franklin*. It was a 130-ton meso-caph, fifty feet long, ten feet across, and powered with four twenty-five-horsepower motors, accommodating a crew of six. The vessel was equipped with a wide variety of scientific instruments. The captain was Don Kazimer, an ex-sub-mariner and a Grumman underwater specialist, and Piccard was the expedition leader.

The Drift Mission got underway July 14, 1969, from West Palm Beach, Florida, accompanied by the support ship *Privateer.* The *Ben Franklin* dove to 1,500 feet, then floated with the current. Piccard worked the mesocaph at varying depths. Thirty-one days and 1,500 miles later, the Drift Mission ended at Halifax, Nova Scotia. The mission was a success in many ways, although the deep scattering layer remained a mystery. The accumulated data took years to evaluate. Magnetic tapes provided sonic "maps" of the ocean floor. NASA received 65,000 photographs of the crew taken by automatic cameras inside the mesocaph.

The Americans beat the French to the Challenger Deep, but a new era of oceanography would star a Frenchman, Jacques-Yves Cousteau. He was born in Saint-André-de-Cubzac, France, in 1910, and it wasn't long before his talents surfaced. When he was eleven, his father brought home blueprints for a marine crane and Jacques built a four-foot model from them. His proud father showed it to an engineer, who noticed that the boy had added an improve-ment to the original design.

Cousteau graduated second in his class at the French naval academy and was accepted for pilot training, but was badly injured in an automobile collision. Doctors wanted to amputate his arm, but Cousteau refused. For nearly a year he could move only one finger on the injured arm.

Jacques Cousteau, inventor of scuba, who ushered in a new age of underwater exploration with his Soucoupe, *a self-propelled deep-diving craft.*

Returning to the Navy at Toulon, he slowly rebuilt his body by swimming in the Mediterranean. In 1936 he took up a new sport called "goggling," the predecessor of scuba diving. Cousteau experimented with devices to extend a diver's time underwater.

After the fall of France, Cousteau reported on German naval activities for the Underground. For his service, Cousteau was awarded the Croix de Guerre and the Légion d'Honneur.

During the war a French naval captain, Yves le Prieur, developed a diving apparatus, a cylinder of compressed air carried on the back of the diver with a hose to a face mask. There was no way, however, to coordinate the air pressure with the water pressure, which limited its use to shallow water. Cousteau went to Paris on forged papers to see Emile Gagnan, who had designed a valve to control the flow of cooking gas. They created the demand regulator, which released air to the diver only when he inhaled, and automatically adjusted to changing water pressure. This was the device that made scuba possible.

Cousteau helped form the French Undersea Research Unit after the war and raised money to buy an old British minesweeper, the *Calypso,* and fit it out as a floating laboratory. Cousteau and a group from the French Navy Group for Undersea Study and Research spent several years on the *Calypso* recovering Greek and Roman treasures. In 1953 this odyssey resulted in the internationally acclaimed book and documentary film *The Silent World.*

To free-dive beyond the depth limitations of scuba equipment, Cousteau designed and built a saucer-shaped underwater craft, the *DS-2,* nicknamed *La Soucoupe* (the diving saucer). The craft, its steel hull encased in a bright yellow fiberglass jacket, was powered and steered by two jet nozzles controlled by the pilot, who with a crewman lay prone on a foam-rubber pad, looking out through a small port. After testing well in shallow dives, the *DS-2* was put aboard the *Calypso* and taken to the Mediterranean. Off Corsica, Cousteau took the vessel down 1,000 feet—more than three times the effective depth of a scuba diver.

In 1962 Cousteau introduced his Continental Shelf Station No. 1 (Conshelf 1), a manned habitat on the ocean floor. Two scientists lived in its cabin for a week, coming out of the habitat with scuba gear to work underwater for hours at a time. Next came Conshelf 2 on Sha'ab Rummi (Roman Reef) in the Red Sea, the first underwater human colony.

Five marine researchers lived in the main structure for a month, working outside for as long as five hours a day in depths up to 100 feet. At an advance station, two divers lived in a mixture of helium and oxygen for a week, diving on compressed air to 363 feet. None of the divers required decompression during the experiment.

La Soucoupe was used as a taxi for the scientists. Compressed air kept out the sea from its dome-shaped hangar. *La Soucoupe* was hoisted to the ceiling and a floor put in place to permit mechanics to work on it unencumbered by scuba gear.

Cousteau and his son Philippe became television stars aboard the *Calypso*. A series of TV specials depicted their diving adventures on a six-year odyssey to the oceans of the world. After the series began in the late 1960s, Cousteau became both the symbol of and spokesman for man's fascination with the underwater world. "Man is just beginning to explore the seas," he said sadly, "and already he has discovered they are dying."

Since the end of World War II, the U.S. Navy has been an increasingly major factor in oceanography. In 1946 a Division of Oceanography was created at the Navy hydrographic office to collect and codify oceanographic information. The Office of Naval Research also was established that year, and it provides the main support in the United States for oceanographic research activities. A number of naval organizations now are involved in oceanography, providing a stream of information and technological advances that have benefited the submarine program in numerous ways.

Underwater technology received worldwide attention in the dramatic search for a hydrogen bomb lost in the ocean off the coast of Spain. A B-52 Stratofortress carrying four H-bombs was refueling in flight on January 16, 1966, when it collided with the tanker and exploded, the debris falling over a large area of land and sea. Lost were four H-bombs with the power of one million tons of TNT, sufficient to atomize southern Spain.

Three of the nuclear bombs were quickly recovered on land. To find the fourth, a massive hunt concentrated on twenty-five square miles of ocean off Palomares. Two deep submersibles were rushed to the scene, the 51-foot *Aluminaut*, capable of working down to 15,000 feet, and the *Alvin*, a 22-foot midget submarine owned by the Office of Naval Research, which could operate to 6,000 feet.

Other equipment used included the two-man submersible Cubmarine, five "acoustic fish," the Ocean Bottom
Scanning Sonar, a Decca radio navigation system for charting
the search from shore, and underwater television cameras
towed on diving sleds. A formidable task lay ahead. Admiral
William S. Guest, in charge of the operation, told the press,
"It isn't like looking for a needle in a haystack. It's like looking for the eye of a needle in a field of haystacks in the dark."

After nearly two months of round-the-clock dives, the
Alvin spotted the missing H-bomb at 2,650 feet, still attached
to its 60-foot-long parachute canopy. Both bomb and canopy
were almost completely buried in loose silt. In an attempt to
hoist the bomb to the surface, it slipped loose, fell to the
bottom, and was lost again. The *Alvin* took several days to
relocate the bomb at 2,800 feet on the edge of a slope.

The CURV (cable-controlled underwater research vessel), its claws monitored by on-board television cameras and
operated remotely from the surface, was called into service,
but by the time it was in position the bomb was gone. The
Alvin relocated the bomb 300 yards away. The CURV was
maneuvered into position to attach cables to the bomb.

Suddenly an ocean current billowed the parachute
canopy, enshrouding the CURV's engines so tightly that it
couldn't move. Admiral Guest ordered the cables winched
tight to see if the CURV could be pulled free. The cables
grew taut, then slackened. The winch slowly reeled in the
cables. The *Alvin* radioed that it saw the CURV, with the
parachute and bomb still attached, 400 feet off the bottom.
The winch started up again, bringing the cables in a few feet
a second. At last the CURV broke the surface, then the parachute appeared, and finally the H-bomb. It was swung
aboard a Navy ship, two months and twenty-one days after it
was lost.

The famed submersible Alvin *being lowered into the water on its search for a lost hydrogen bomb off the coast of Spain (1966).*

During the underwater search for the missing H-bomb, the public became familiar with deep research vessels (D/RVs) through the work of the *Aluminaut* and the *Alvin*. There are some one hundred D/RVs in the world, half of them in the United States. Most were built by aerospace companies, and they look it. With their brightly colored acrylic domes and large external mechanical arms, they would seem as much at home on Mars as on the ocean floor. They are submersibles, not submarines, and require surface support vessels. D/RVs are used to make observations and gather samples, often at great depths. Although they share a basic purpose, no two D/RVs are alike.

Other D/RVs include a number of Perry Submersibles, the Cubmarines, designed for observation and salvage work at mid-depth ranges on the continental shelf. The Shell Oil Company uses its Shelf Diver to inspect underwater pipelines. The vessel has twenty-five viewports, two drills for core and rock, a mechanical arm, and television cameras.

A D/RV that has been used extensively by the Navy is *Deep Star 4000*, designed by Cousteau and built under his guidance by Westinghouse. The 18-foot, nine-ton vessel can operate at depths down to 4,000 feet. Westinghouse built a successor, the 36-foot, thirty-two-ton *Deep Star 20,000* for searches down to 20,000 feet.

Cousteau built *Diving Saucer SP-3000* in 1970 for his own use, a 20-foot, twelve-ton D/RV capable of operating at 9,000-foot depths. An unusual D/RV was designed and built by the Navy, the sixty-six-inch acrylic sphere *Nemo* that sits atop disks containing its life-support system. *Nemo* operates on a cable anchored to the ocean floor, and two crewmen can winch the bell up or down. The Navy also designed and built *Deep View*, the first D/RV with its entire bow section capped with a glass hemisphere. The 16½-foot, nearly six-ton vessel is propelled by four electric motors and can dive to 1,500 feet.

The Navy's first deep sea rescue vehicle, the DSRV-1, was launched in 1970 to search out a downed nuclear submarine, link itself to the submarine's escape hatch, and take the crew to the surface, twenty-four at a time. The vessel is 50 feet long with a torpedo-shaped fiberglass hull, and can operate 3,500 feet down. In 1971 Lockheed built the DSRV-2, operational to 5,000 feet. Both DSRVs can be transported by air and can be carried on a nuclear submarine, which can launch and recover them without surfacing. Both soon were called to the rescue in an underwater tragedy.

The *Johnson-Sea-Link* was a twenty-three-foot, nine-ton D/RV designed by Edwin Link and financed by industrialist

The U.S. Navy's deep sea rescue vehicle, DSRV-1.

J. Seward Johnson. On June 17, 1973, Link's son, Clayton, and three other men were in the D/RV off Key West working at a depth of 360 feet near a sunken destroyer. Suddenly a strong current swept the *Sea-Link* off course and entangled it among the wreck's cables and debris. The pilot, Archibald Menzies, couldn't get the D/RV free and radioed for help.

Five hours later the Navy submarine rescue vessel *Tringa* was in position, but the crew of the *Sea-Link* was having trouble with the air supply. The *Sea-Link* had two compartments, two men in each, with no access from one compartment to another. The "scrubbers" that purified the air weren't working properly, and Link and Menzies in their separate compartments made emergency repairs.

Deep-sea divers made three futile attempts to reach the stricken vessel, once coming within ten feet before being driven back by the current and debris. The submarine *Amberjack* arrived the next morning with two small submersibles. They were launched, but one malfunctioned and the other was unable to reach the *Sea-Link*. A Navy diving bell was flown in, and two scuba divers took her down but couldn't reach the D/RV either.

The oceanographic research ship *A. B. Wood* arrived and lowered a closed-circuit television camera. Menzies saw it and talked it into position over the radio. The camera was hauled up, a grapple hook was attached to the camera cable, and relowered. Again Menzies talked it into position, and a few minutes later the *Sea-Link* was hauled to the surface. Menzies and one other survived; Link and another crewman were dead from carbon-dioxide poisoning.

In another incident, a Navy unmanned CURV was flown to the rescue in October 1973 when the 29-foot submersible *Pisces* sank in 1,375 feet of water off the coast of Ireland. The CURV, similar to the one that pulled up the lost H-bomb, dived and was directed from the surface by its closed-circuit television camera. It attached a cable to the *Pisces* and it was hoisted to the surface. The two crewmen were saved, despite a nearly seventy-six-hour ordeal.

An important scientific study was launched in 1974: Project FAMOUS, an acronym for the French-American Mid-Ocean Undersea Study. The subject: the largest physical feature of the earth, a 40,000-mile ridge that girdles the globe and bisects the Atlantic Ocean. In the valley that runs along the ridge, scientists believe, volcanic activity forms new seabed. Perhaps the findings of Project FAMOUS would link this volcanic activity to the phenomenon of continental drift. Geologists aren't sure whether in continental drift the earth's plates are pushed apart by the surge of lava or pulled apart by other forces. If the plates were pushed, Project FAMOUS would find telltale signs, buckled crust and piles of lava.

The site of Project FAMOUS was a section of the range and rift valley 250 miles south of the Azores. The American team used the *Alvin*, recently refitted with a titanium hull that extended its operational range to 12,000 feet. The French used the bathyscaph *L'Archimede* and the *Cyana*, once Cousteau's *Diving Saucer SP 3000*.

After repeated dives to the seabed 9,000 feet below, the scientists found a variety of lava formations in a 500-foot section of the valley indicating recent volcanic eruptions, but nothing suggesting seabed movement. Instead, there were many fissures and rips, indicating that the bottom had been literally wrenched apart. An unusually large amount of sea life was observed, and samples from the bottom were rich in iron and manganese. This suggested to the scientists that there might be thermal springs in the rift valley, but a search didn't locate them.

During the summerlong exploration, the three submersibles collected a mass of samples and data. The *Alvin*
alone brought back 867 pounds of rocks and took some
17,000 of the 50,000 exhibition photographs. Project
FAMOUS was a major step forward in man's understanding
of the underwater environment.

9 | Room Aboard for Everything But a Mistake

A nuclear submarine is incredibly complex, wondrously sensitive, and awesomely powerful. It is also numbingly expensive. A Los Angeles–class fast-attack submarine costs $750 million; a prototype of a new class may cost twice that much. And the gestation period of a prototype is long. First, the Navy decides what role a new class of submarines must fulfill, the weapons and sensors to be placed aboard, and the performance standards to be met. From that point to a finished prototype may take a decade.

Until the mid-1960s, submarines had one primary role: to attack enemy naval and merchant ships. That still is a primary role, but new roles have been added. Submarines capable of launching ballistic and cruise missiles now can strike directly at targets in the enemy's homeland. And submarines can locate and attack enemy submarines. Other submarine roles include general patrol duties and clandestine special operations. The particular role of a submarine determines its design.

Innovations incorporated into a new class have to be tested, not simply for individual performance but in relation to everything else on the submarine, because everything on a submarine affects everything else. Electric Boat says that a new submarine design requires as many as 2,000 working drawings. Blueprints from these drawings, if placed end to end, would make a strip 250 miles long. Finally, submarine construction involves some seven million parts, many of them unique in design and manufacture.

There is more science packed into a submarine than any other warship. To complicate matters, the space tolerances are infinitely more demanding. However, the Navy likes to say, "There is room for everything aboard a submarine except a mistake."

Design of a submarine involves four stages: inception, conceptual design, contract design, and working drawings. It starts in the Office of the Chief of Naval Operations (OPNAV), where the number and types of ships and submarines necessary to maintain an adequate naval force are determined. OPNAV proposes to the secretary of the Navy an annual shipbuilding program, usually involving both new construction and modernization of existing hulls. A request for a new submarine design originates in the Ship Characteristics Board of OPNAV.

Once a new design has been initiated, exploratory studies are made of available data and the performance characteristics are determined. Many design feasibility studies are made, and from these develops a set of tentative characteristics.

Then a set of drawings and data sheets is prepared showing the principal features of the basic design based on the approved submarine characteristics. During this stage the size and shape of the hull are determined. Models are tested to find a hull with the optimum maneuvering characteristics, the correct propeller design, and the shaft horsepower required.

This information is now checked, refined, and redrawn in greater detail. These are the contract drawings and ship specifications that become a part of the contract with the shipbuilder. The shipbuilder prepares the working drawings from which the submarine will be built.

Hull design is central to the submarine performance. At the end of World War II, the state of the art was the long, narrow, highly streamlined hull of the German Type XXI patrol submarine, and it was quickly adopted by the U.S., British, Russian, and French Navies. But as propulsion systems improved, control problems developed at speeds in excess of twelve knots. The submarine would begin to pitch to the point where, under certain conditions, control could be lost completely.

A breakthrough came in 1953, inspired by the aeronautical principles of the blimp. The new design was first used on the American diesel-electric experimental submarine *Albacore*. The shorter, fatter, more maneuverable hull was symmetrical along its long axis, like a torpedo.

The *Albacore* also incorporated sail planes and was the first submarine that could "fly" like an airplane, making tightly banked curves and, reportedly, even underwater loops. The hull was stable at all speeds, and its 15,000 horsepower could drive it submerged at speeds in excess of thirty-three knots, unheard of at the time. The hull shape also provided greater internal storage space and a multideck layout. Most submarines among Western countries now have a variation of the *Albacore* hull.

There are two overriding considerations in hull design: a submerged submarine must have neutral buoyancy, and it must have a center of gravity lying below its center of buoyancy.

The center of buoyancy depends on the volume of water the submarine displaces, and is controlled by varying the volume of displacement. On the surface the main ballast tanks are filled with air; when submerged the tanks are filled with water. Filling the tanks with air moves the center of buoyancy above the center of gravity; the reverse happens when the tanks are filled with water. The deeper a submarine dives, the greater the outside water pressure, and the pressure actually compresses the hull, with a resulting loss of buoyancy of several tons.

Designers are increasingly concerned with the hull's metallurgy, thickness, and reinforcement, for these determine how deep a submarine can dive. Depth gives a submarine a greater margin of safety in high-speed maneuvers, and protection from detection.

Hydrodynamic efficiency is another factor. A submerged submarine is impeded by the total effect of three forms of drag: skin friction, form drag, and appendage drag. The *Albacore*'s hull greatly reduced skin friction, even with a cylindrical midbody. Skin friction is directly proportional to surface area; the bigger the hull, the greater the drag.

Form drag accounts for only 2 to 4 percent of the total drag on an *Albacore* hull, but that's sufficient to concern the designers. Form drag is sharply increased by anything protruding from the hull, which is why the deck impediments of World War II submarines are gone. Built into the hull of a nuclear submarine are dozens of hatches, cleats, connections, and other items.

Streamlining has gone about as far as current research can take it, and designers now concentrate on the nature of the hull surface. Special paints can reduce friction, which means higher speeds. Speed also can be increased for short periods by releasing polymers around the hull.

Russian designers cover the hulls of the Oscar-class submarines with tiles that are believed to provide acoustic absorption and boundary-layer pressure equalization. There have been reports that the Russian developments came from studying dolphins and killer whales, whose skins help them adjust to boundary-layer pressure changes.

Marine mammal research may have led to fins or hydroplanes that change shape as the submarine's speed changes. The submarines had bulbous bows, shaped like the nose of a whale, and sails that resemble the fins of marine mammals.

Fins, or hydroplanes, are the major control surfaces of a submarine. The designer strives to attain the perfect compromise between maneuverability and low drag. The size, shape, and location of fins have changed over the years. The early Holland submarines had no forward hydroplanes; later submarines incorporated them to maintain an even keel in a dive. U.S. nuclear submarines have fins on their sails, but starting with the new *San Juan* they are gone, replaced by retractable hull fins.

Wherever the fins are placed, the submarine must meet critical maneuverability standards: turning within less than four times the submarine's length, and ascending and descending at rates of several hundred feet a minute.

The stern design also receives the close attention of the designers, particularly the correlation of hull shape, propeller, and control surfaces. During World War II the stern control surfaces were aft of the propeller. Most submarines have horizontal control surfaces forward of the propeller. In a variation on this, Los Angeles– and Ohio-class nuclear submarines have vertical endplates on the aft horizontal fins, improving control and housing hydrophones.

Walrus-class Swedish and Dutch submarines incorporate X-shaped appendages, which give greater operating control and are quieter. Whatever the placement, the complex relationship between steering and diving functions of the hydroplanes necessitates a computer-assisted operation.

To avoid enemy sonar a submarine must run quietly, but there are other design considerations in avoiding detection. A smaller submarine presents a smaller sonar target, but it takes a large submarine to house modern weapon and sensor systems. The hull can be shaped to diffuse sonar, but this can sharply increase drag. Sound-absorbing tiles are the most promising development, and tiles will be incorporated in the next generation of American attack submarines.

There are four main types of hulls in use today: single hull, saddle tank, double hull, and multihull. Single-hull submarines have their main ballast tanks mounted within the hull itself or, as with the Los Angeles–class submarines, mounted externally at either end of the pressure hull. The main ballast tanks in saddle-tank submarines are mounted externally as additions to the pressure hull with free-flooding holes at the bottom and vents on the top. The British Navy uses saddle tanks in its Oberon class.

Multihull submarines offer exceptional hull strength but are expensive and difficult to construct. Russian Typhoon-class ballistic-missile submarines reportedly have multihulls. Experts believe that these huge submarines have two complete, interconnected pressure hulls, each with crew quarters and propulsion machinery; a third smaller section under the sail serves as the command and control center.

All submarine hulls are stiffened by ring frames and supported by traverse bulkheads. Both ends of the pressure hull have domed end-closures. All hulls, however, must have a ballast keel. The keel is mounted within the hull on double- and multihull submarines, externally on single and saddle-tank hulls.

Hulls for American submarines are made of high-yield steel. Other countries have experimented with other materials: titanium, aluminum, even glass. Two classes of Russian submarines, Alfa and Mike, are built of titanium, stronger than steel and nonmagnetic. They cannot be detected by airborne MAD (magnetic anomaly detector) equipment or coils laid on the seabed. Titanium is exceedingly difficult to weld, but the Russian metallurgists apparently have mastered the technique.

Alfas are said to be capable of submerged speeds in excess of forty-two knots and can dive to somewhere between 2,000 and 3,000 feet, greater depths than any current American submarine can handle. The Russians, who poured billions into submarine research, refer to the Alfa as the "Golden Fish."

All current American nuclear-powered submarines use a pressurized-water reactor to superheat water under high pressure to prevent it from boiling, and send it to a steam generator. Heat energy is transferred in the generator from the superheated water in the primary circuit to unpressurized water in the secondary circuit. This produces steam, which is passed to the turbine. After driving the turbine, the steam goes into a series of condensers where it becomes water and is returned to the steam generator for recycling.

A constant flow of seawater is used by condensers for cooling. This is provided mechanically if the submarine is underway at speed; pumps are used under other conditions.

A crewman runs a systems check on one of the sixteen missile tubes aboard the nuclear-powered Daniel Boone.

But the pumps are noisy. In search of a quieter system, designers have tested alternative coolants. The *Seawolf* was fitted in the late 1950s with a liquid-sodium-cooled reactor. This gave excellent heat transference, but had service problems. If the sodium wasn't kept constantly heated, it solidified and ruined the primary circuit pipes. The plant was plagued with steam leaks, and finally was replaced by a water-cooled system.

The Russians seem to have better luck with liquid-metal cooling systems. Alfa-class submarines reportedly use a liquid-metal-cooled reactor. Alfas also have unmanned, automated engine rooms, cutting the amount of reactor shielding needed.

Modern propellers have as many as seven blades, which run at a very low number of revolutions per minute. Despite design refinements, propellers are a major source of noise, and each propeller design produces a unique sound. The nationality and class of a submarine can be identified by sophisticated sonar devices from its characteristic sound "signature."

Whatever the refinements, the noise problem cannot be entirely eliminated; a moving submarine creates some noise and leaves a wake. In the wake are thermal and ultraviolet radiation disruptions and trails of dying microorganisms, all of which can be detected by sophisticated sensors.

A submarine-launched cruise missile (SLCM) is a pilotless aircraft propelled by an air-breathing engine that operates aerodynamically within the earth's atmosphere. In flight the cruise missile is controlled and guided either by an on-board computer or remotely by satellite.

A submarine-launched ballistic missile (SLBM), however, is a rocket, propelled into space by one or more boosters. The thrust is terminated at an early stage, and the missile follows a trajectory that is governed by gravity and aerodynamic drag, although minor corrections can be made in flight.

Ballistic missiles can carry a greater payload over a much greater distance than can a cruise missile, but they sacrifice pinpoint accuracy and total control. A cruise missile, for example, can fly close to the ground, hugging the terrain to avoid radar detection.

The first cruise missiles aboard submarines were launched through torpedo tubes. These included the Sub-Harpoon antiship missile and the Tomahawk, which could attack both ships and land targets. The Navy then decided that the missiles took up too much space in the torpedo room, and they were placed in vertically mounted launching tubes between the bow sonar and the forward end of the pressure hull. The SM39 Exocet, a French antiship missile fired from torpedo tubes, proved effective in the 1982 Falkland Islands war.

In the 1950s the U.S. Navy introduced carrier-based AJ-1 Savages, capable of carrying the Mark V atomic bomb. This spurred the Soviets to begin a crash program to build attack and cruise missile submarines.

In the last months of World War II the Germans were considering using submarines to launch V-2 rockets against American targets. Nazi submarine and rocket technology helped both the U.S. and Russia advance the concept of a ballistic-missile submarine. The Soviet Navy was first. Diesel-powered submarines armed with three SS-N-3 missiles came into service in 1958. Crude by today's standards, a submarine had to surface to launch missiles.

The U.S. Navy countered with Polaris, a dramatic breakthrough in missile system technology. Developed by Admiral W. F. Rayborn and Lockheed, the Polaris met its two initial requirements: the use of a solid propellant and the capability of underwater launching. Also incorporated in the Polaris system: lightweight reentry vehicles, miniaturized inertial guidance, miniaturized nuclear and thermonuclear warheads, cold-gas launch techniques, and submarine inertial navigation. When the Polaris system went into service in November 1960, it changed the entire nature of strategic warfare.

The Soviets weren't long in catching up. A new missile, the SS-N-5, could be launched from a submerged submarine, and the SS-N-6 was small enough for a Yankee-class submarine to carry sixteen. This brought parity with U.S. ballistic submarines. The SS-N-8 missile had a range of 4,800 nautical miles, by far the longest at that time. The next development, the SS-N-9, gave the Soviet Navy a multiple, independently targetable reentry vehicle (MIRV).

Another major Soviet advancement was the SS-N-18, a missile with a range of 4,300 nautical miles. The U.S. didn't match it until the Trident II became operational ten years later. Then came the SS-N-20 and SS-N-23, both with ranges of 4,800 nautical miles, and carried by Typhoon and Delta IV submarines.

The submarine is a mobile launch pad, but in order for a missile launch to be effective, the captain needs to know the precise position, velocity, and depth of his submarine. The navigation system transmits this data continuously to fire control. Inertial navigation (SINS) records every movement of the submarine in relation to a theoretical table platform, and can be updated with input from loran or optical observations.

Fire control prepares and fires the missiles. It sets up the missile guidance system inertial platform, determines true launch bearing, stores and computes target data, and passes data to the missile guidance computer.

The launch system stores, protects, and ejects the missiles, which are enclosed in capsules stowed inside shock-protected, water-tight launch tubes. Some missiles are ejected by compressed air, others by steam.

About ninety feet after the missile clears

A Poseidon missile being launched from the USS Daniel Boone. *The sub's antenna is visible at right.*

the tube, the first-stage motor ignites to propel the missile through the ocean surface, into the atmosphere, and up into space. When the first stage has been expended, it separates and falls away, and the second-stage motor ignites and propels the missile. The Trident and the Russian SS-N-20 and SS-N-23 missiles have a third-stage motor.

The missile's navigation equipment continuously measures linear acceleration from its inertial system, altering the missile's trajectory to counteract any outside forces such as wind that affect acceleration. When the missile arrives at the correct velocity, altitude, and position for the target, the bus carrying the reentry vehicles (RVs) separates from the final stage and continues its flight. Individual RVs are dropped off according to instructions fed into the missile's computer just before the launch. The warheads reenter the atmosphere at steep angles, a special coating absorbing the heat. Decoys are released with the warheads to deceive antimissile systems.

The first SLBMs had a single reentry vehicle containing the warhead. Advanced technology led to multiple reentry vehicles (MRVs). The warheads were all aimed at the same target, but were spread out in a shotgun pattern. The next step was the development of independently targetable reentry vehicles (MIRVs), which could be dropped off the reentry vehicle at different points to hit individual targets. State-of-the-art missiles now incorporate maneuverable reentry vehicles (MARVs), which can steer precisely to the target independent of the accuracy of the launch.

Warhead accuracy is measured in terms of "circular area probable" (cep). This is the radius of a circle centered on the point of aim into which 50 percent of all warheads launched can be expected to hit. The first SLBMs were reasonably inaccurate because they were totally dependent on the submarine's SINS, but there has been steady improvement. Polaris had a cep of 0.5 nautical mile; Poseidon, 0.3; Trident I, 0.23. That means a submarine can launch a Trident missile at a target nearly 5,000 miles away and half of the warheads will hit within some 500 yards of dead center.

The increasing degree of accuracy of ballistic missiles has brought about a change in defense planning. The early missiles were limited to area targets, such as cities and large military installations. But the newer MARV missiles, capable of accuracy measured in tens of feet, could be effective against such small targets as enemy missile silos. The comparative accuracy of competitors' ballistic missiles has a profound effect on the balance of power.

Trident I carries a similar payload to that of the Poseidon but with a much greater range, 4,230 nautical miles compared to Poseidon's 2,500. This permits a much larger area of operations. Trident I owes its increased range to an aerospike on the nose of the missile, which reduces drag by 50 percent; to improved fuel; and to a third-stage motor.

Trident II was designed for greater accuracy, and the nearly forty-six-foot missile can carry fourteen RVs, al-

Workers in a missile tube aboard the James Madison *suggest the awesome size of the Trident missile—46 feet long.*

though the SALT II agreement imposes an RV limit of ten. Twenty Ohio-class submarines reportedly will each carry twenty Trident IIs. Four British submarines also are receiving Trident IIs.

In the age of missiles, torpedoes still are an important part of a submarine's arsenal. They have been modernized in an attempt to meet the new standards of naval warfare. Torpedo speed is a problem. The U.S. Mark 46 torpedo travels at forty knots, but so does a Russian Alfa-class submarine, which eliminates the possibility of a stern shot. A program called Advanced Capability (ADCAP) reportedly will raise the speed of the Mark 48 torpedo to fifty-five knots.

Great progress has been made in torpedo guidance systems. Torpedoes now incorporate a sonar transducer that switches from passive to active automatically once the target

Missile tubes ready for loading with Trident C-4 missiles on the USS Ohio.

responds to the attack. Guidance wires link the torpedo to the submarine and can both control the torpedo and pass sonar information to the submarine's fire control system.

But the torpedo is far from being a perfect weapon. In the Falkland Islands war, both the British and the Argentinean Navies reported numerous instances of malfunctioning torpedoes. It is ironic that while the Whitehead torpedo was developed before there was a submarine capable of launching it, torpedoes now trail submarines in performance.

Submarines still lay mines, now launching them from their torpedo tubes. Planes, helicopters, and surface ships also lay mines, but submarines excel when the mines need to be laid secretly and precisely. Conversely, modern mines are effective antisubmarine weapons, triggering on a submarine's acoustic, magnetic, or electrical signature. Particularly lethal is the U.S. Navy's Captor (encapsulated torpedo), which lies on the bottom and fires a torpedo.

A submerged submarine is blind, totally dependent on its sensors, particularly its sonar. SSNs and SSBNs have a large sonar mounted in the bow and, just aft, large arrays of conformal sonar. Underwater listening devices called hydrophones are on the bow, amidships, and near the stern. Among other things, the hull hydrophones monitor the submarine's own noises. When a submarine leaves port, a surface ship checks its noise level, but new noises can develop at sea. If undetected, they can attract the enemy.

Active sonar devices transmit acoustic pulses at audio frequency levels at a rate that ranges from 12.5 to 700 milliseconds, depending on oceanic conditions. Highly sophisticated equipment assists sonar operators in assimilating and processing the sonar signals. Large numbers of transducers mounted in arrays make up active sonar systems. In

Torpedo room of the USS John Adams.

the bow, cylindrical arrays electronically form a beam, giving directional resolution. A shift in the return signal indicates a moving target.

Several problems are inherent in active sonar: noise generated by the parent submarine is picked up along with incoming signals; changing oceanic conditions often distort the beams; and sonar signals can be picked up by enemy sonar.

Los Angeles–class submarines carry the BQQ-5 active sonar system spherically mounted in their bows. This system employs the submarine active detection system (SADS) and is integrated with other systems on board, including the mine detection avoidance sonar (MIDAS) and systems to enable the submarine to operate beneath the polar ice cap.

Current sonar research focuses on increasing its ability to detect, while reducing its revealing signature. One development is spread-spectrum transmission in which the signal is varied over a preprogrammed transmission band, reducing the chance of the enemy picking it out of the background of oceanic noises.

Passive sonar, involving no transmission, no chance of betraying the submarine's position, is precisely tuned to pick up submarine and ship signatures through hydrophones. The signals are processed by powerful computers and analyzed by specialists. The U.S. Navy has a clear lead in this arcane science.

Passive sonars usually use the same arrays as the active sonar system. Towed arrays often are employed, comprising as many as several hundred hydrophones. Los Angeles–class SSNs use the BQQ-25, a towed array with a 2,624-foot cable. One advantage of a towed array is its unique ability to scan rearward. This is countered by several disadvantages: the submarine must slow down and run in a straight line while operating a towed array, and its size makes it a problem to store on board. Russian submarines also use a variety of towed arrays.

Once, the submarine's only sensor was its periscope. Submarines normally have two, one for general use and a smaller one employed while attacking surface ships. The modern periscope is a highly sophisticated instrument capable of many tasks. Among its equipment: a microprocessor to estimate bearing and range and to feed the information into the fire control system; a laser rangefinder accurate to within three feet; artificial horizon sextants to take quick sights to update the submarine's inertial navigational system; sensors to warn of electronic threats; thermal imagers for night or bad-weather use; and still and television cameras.

Like everything else aboard a submarine, the periscopes involve compromises. To use his periscopes, a commander must put his submarine in a dangerous position. The exposed part of the periscope makes a wake that can be seen or picked up by radar. At speeds above ten knots, the periscope vibrates, and the longer the tube, the greater the vibration. But a short tube brings the submarine that much closer to the surface and its attendant perils.

Other sensors poke out of a submarine's sail. There are radio direction-finding antennas and radar to search the sea and sky. Adding in air intakes and the antennas for various communication equipment, a Los Angeles–class submarine has twelve masts. When the submarine submerges, the masts retract into the sail and are covered by remotely controlled hatches, reducing turbulence and noise.

Through World War II a submarine had to surface to use its radio. There was no way to communicate with a submerged submarine, but a submarine couldn't stay submerged for very long anyway. Today's submarines can stay submerged for months at a time, and surfacing involves the risk of detection. This has spurred developments in radio technology.

Radio waves are weakened as they pass through water, and the higher the frequency, the greater the loss in strength. And radio waves, like sound waves, are distorted underwater.

Radio signals of very low frequency (3kHz to 30kHz) can reach a submarine fifty feet below the surface. To receive VLF broadcasts, a submarine will either trail a long wire antenna, or a loop antenna mounted on a buoy. The problem is that letting out the wire or buoy creates noise.

The U.S. Navy has seven shore-based VLF transmitting stations, NATO two, and Britain one. The Russians have ten. The antennas for VLF stations are big, expensive, and vulnerable to attack.

A further development is radio communication at extremely low frequencies (300Hz to 3kHz), which can be received by a submarine at 500 feet. Innovative new equipment reportedly can transmit successfully to 1,300 feet. ELF, as this is called, is practically impervious to either jamming or the effects of a nuclear explosion, which makes it particularly suited for communicating with second-strike SSBNs.

However, the information transmission rate is extremely low. The U.S. Navy's Austere ELF system takes fifteen minutes to transmit a three-letter group, although highly compressed codes make it possible to send a lot of information using three-letter groups. ELF systems also need huge transmitting antennas.

The U.S. Navy set up a test facility in the 1970s at Clam Lake, Wisconsin, which used telephone poles to support an X-shaped antenna with arms seven miles long. Transmitting at a power of only two watts, it was able to reach a submarine 427 feet beneath 33 feet of Arctic ice. The Clam Lake facility now is used in conjunction with a similar installation at K. I. Sawyer Air Force base in Michigan to provide a full operation system.

The primary meas of communicating with fleet submarines now is the TACAMO (take charge and move out) system. Two squadrons of Lockheed EC-130AQ aircraft, one in the Atlantic, one in the Pacific, act as radio relays between the command and the SSBNs. One aircraft is over each ocean at any given time, and another is on fifteen minutes' notice on the ground.

The planes have a communications center with a variety of equipment that can transmit in VLF, LF, HF, and UHF bands. To transmit on VLF, a wire antenna more than six miles long is trailed from the aircraft. A new plane, the E-6, is taking over the TACAMO system.

Buoys of various types are used as relays in communicating with submerged submarines. The SSQ-86 (XN-1) is a down-link communication (DCL) buoy that transmits a programmed message to a submarine without requiring the submarine to reveal its position.

The DCL is mounted in a standard sonobuoy and can be launched from an aircraft or surface ship. The buoy transmits its message (limited to four groups of three characters) once near the surface, descends to a predetermined depth, transmits a second time, pauses for five minutes, transmits a third time, then self-destructs. The entire process takes some seventeen minutes.

Laser has a potential for communicating with submarines. There is an optical window in the blue-green part of the spectrum that allows laser transmissions to penetrate to considerable depths. Considerable power is needed, for such transmissions and satellites can't carry the necessary generating equipment. A way around this is to use a laser on the ground to bounce the signal off a space-based mirror. This way, transmissions could be made 300 times faster than with an ELF system, although the receiving submarine would have to be closer to the surface.

Submarines can run at periscope depth, using a mast-mounted antenna to beam messages off satellites. Such transmissions are hard to detect from ground monitoring stations, although they can be detected by aircraft with special detection equipment, and by other satellites.

Transmitting buoys, such as the U.S. Navy's BRT-1, can relay messages from a submarine to bases on shore or to surface ships. The buoy can be preset to delay the transmission from fifteen minutes to an hour, permitting the submarine to clear the area, lessening the chance of detection.

It is exceptionally difficult for one submerged submarine to communicate with another. Under certain circumstances acoustic underwater telephones can be used, but usually intercommunication between submarines involves sending the message to the base to be relayed to the other submarine by one of the various communication channels.

Communication technology continually improves, but a ballistic submarine still must often operate on its own, completely out of touch for long periods of time from its command, other submarines, and surface ships and aircraft. Although he cannot fire missiles unless ordered to do so, the commander must make many combat decisions himself.

10 The United States No Longer Has Mastery of the Seas

Ballistic submarine bases are, by necessity, large, and their locations cannot be kept secret. The U.S. has two—Kings Bay, Georgia, and Bangor, Washington—to support, maintain, repair, and refit SSBNs and their missiles, and to provide necessary services to their crews.

The oldest base, now closed, was Holy Loch, Scotland. President Eisenhower met with Prime Minister Sir Anthony Douglas-Home in the early 1950s and negotiated permission to establish a submarine repair facility in British waters to replace the submarine facility at Rota, Spain. Holy Loch, just north of Glasgow, was selected because it provided easy access to the strategic waters of the eastern Atlantic.

The submarine tender *Proteus* and a Polaris missile support ship took up residence at Holy Loch early in 1961.

By 1985 Holy Loch was a large base with a floating dry dock and the headquarters of Commander Submarine Squadron 14. More than 600 patrols sailed from the base, which was designated Site 1 Holy Loch. Site 1 was the abbreviated name of the U.S. Navy's Fleet Ballistic Submarine Refit Site 1, and some 1,600 Navy personnel are stationed there.

Holy Loch had been described as an "industrial Las Vegas, available to 'customers' twenty-four hours a day, 365 days a year." The base averaged twenty-three refits and some 9,400 repairs annually. A saying at Holy Loch: "We can fix everything over here except the crack of dawn."

The next base was Bangor, the 6,929-acre site of a former torpedo station annex on Puget Sound. Construction began in late 1974 and was completed a decade later. The base has nearly 5,000 military personnel and employs some 3,000 civilians. Bangor houses several commands: Naval Submarine Base, Trident Refit Facility, Trident Training Facility, and Strategic Weapons Facility, Pacific.

An officer stationed at Bangor says, "For the first time, if a man really wants to, he can put in almost an entire Navy career here. He could complete a three-year submarine tour and then come ashore at one of a number of Trident activities on base, or serve at the nearby Keyport Torpedo Station, or the Puget Sound Naval Shipyard in Bremerton. If the sailor likes it here, he can put down some real roots and become an active member of the community. I think we're going to have a more stable Navy because of people who elect to do things like that."

The naval bases at New London, Connecticut, and Charleston, South Carolina, service fast-attack submarines and the earlier SSBNs but can't accommodate Ohio-class

Tridents. In anticipation of this problem, the Navy decided to expand its facilities at Kings Bay, near Savannah on the Georgia coast. In 1980 it was designated the Atlantic base for Trident submarines, and became fully operational late in 1989. Kings Bay is the home base for Submarine Squadron 16. Like Bangor, Kings Bay contains training and refit facilities.

Everything at these bases is geared to the schedule of the Tridents: a seventy-five-day deployment followed by a twenty-five-day refit period, one week of which is taken up by the blue-gold crew changeover. This allows base personnel only eighteen days for all refit work. Meeting this tight schedule requires round-the-clock work seven days a week.

Good management and reliable equipment at these facilities enable the Navy to keep 65 percent of its Trident submarines at sea at all times, an improvement on the 45 percent for earlier classes. By contrast, the Russian Navy with more SSBNs is only able to keep 13 percent of them on patrol at the same time.

Under a NATO commitment, the French have two SSBNs constantly on patrol, the British, one. NATO's SSBNs are operated by three different navies under three separate national controls, the U.S., Britain, and France. Each country retains control over its own SLBM warheads.

If Russia should attack Western Europe, it would face a nuclear submarine force. Britain and France, individually or in concert, could inflict a destructive retaliatory attack on Russian land. The British SSBNs are based at Faslane, on the Gare Loch off the River Clyde in Scotland, the French at Brest.

SSBN bases are impossible to hide, and submarine arrivals and departures are closely monitored by satellite and other electronic devices. British SSBNs go to sea in full view of anyone who cares to watch through the narrows at Rhu just north of Helensburgh; the French have a similar situation at Brest. Such narrows are called "choke points" by submariners, and they have a strategic importance.

After passing a choke point a submarine going out or coming in from patrol is easily detectable by satellite in the relatively shallow waters of the continental shelf. Once clear of the shelf, though, an SSBN dives deep and travels at top speed to its patrol area, making sure that it isn't being followed by enemy SSNs. On station, an SSBN will cruise at about three knots, varying its depth to match prevailing oceanic conditions to find the convergence zone where it is safe from enemy sonar. However, it risks detection when it rises near the surface to communicate or update its inertial navigation system.

A huge, Soviet-era Oscar-class cruise-missile submarine.

The Russian Navy understandably regards its ballistic-missile fleet as its most valuable asset, and the U.S. Navy's fleet as a major threat. Military observers believe that the Russian surface fleet was designed primarily to protect the SSBN fleet, although independent forays may be a secondary capability. As evidence of this, the Russian Navy didn't have an aircraft carrier until the recent past.

Early Soviet SSBNs, the Yankee class, patrolled close to the coast of the United States because their missiles had a limited range. In October 1986 a missile exploded aboard a Yankee, forcing it to surface some 750 nautical miles from Washington, D.C. The 1,600-nautical-mile range of the missiles aboard the Yankees enabled them to threaten such targets as the East Coast Strategic Air Command bases.

In the Far East, Russian SSBNs concentrate in the Sea of Okhotsk; to the west, in the Barents Sea. This compels the U.S. Navy and its allies to send submarines, surface ships, and antisubmarine aircraft to these areas. The Russian SSBN base at Polyarnyi on the Kola Peninsula apparently is too small for Typhoon-class submarines but handles Yankees and Deltas. A new base with protective pens is said to be ready at Gremikha. Russian SSBNs in the Far East are based at Vladivostok and at Petropavlovsk on the Kamchatka Peninsula.

Submarines operating out of Vladivostok have a choke point in the Kunashir Passage to the north of Japan. The Russian Baltic fleet has a choke point between the Danish island of Zealand and the Swedish coast.

In the Mediterranean, the choke points are the Bosporus, around the Aegean Islands, in the Aegean Straits of Kithira and Kárpathos, in the Sicilian Channel, and in the Straits of Gibraltar.

One of the most dramatic developments of the post–World War II period was the growth of the naval strength of the former Soviet Union. From the end of the war until the early 1970s, the United States maintained unquestioned naval supremacy. This gave great flexibility to American foreign policy and provided one of the West's primary shields against Soviet aggression.

A diesel-powered Tango-class submarine in the Russian fleet.

The Soviet Navy concentrated on building up its submarine force in the belief that it could achieve strategic goals in war at sea despite constantly improving antisubmarine weapons. Submarines also were a relatively inexpensive and rapid means of increasing Soviet naval power. From 1945 to 1955 more than 450 diesel attack submarines were built; then the Soviets concentrated on nuclear-powered submarines.

A damaged Russian Victor-class submarine after colliding with a merchant ship.

The Soviet submarine program was described in a 1988 U.S. Department of Defense report, *Soviet Military Power: An Assessment of the Threat,* as "the world's largest strategic missile submarine force" with the majority of its submarines armed with intercontinental-range missiles "that can reach North America from Soviet ports and coastal waters."

The Soviet naval policy was summed up succinctly in the late 1980s by S. G. Gorshkov, Admiral of the Fleet of the Soviet Union and full member of the Central Committee of the Communist Party: "The flag of the Soviet Navy flies over the oceans of the world. Sooner or later the United States will have to understand it no longer has mastery of the seas."

The U.S. Navy's submarine fleet is armed with a mix of Poseidon and Trident missiles. The Navy does not discuss the SSBN patrol areas, but certain assumptions can be made. The range of the Trident permits submarines to

The Mike-class Russian sub, used to test developments in propulsion.
This is one of the latest Russian designs.

patrol in the Atlantic, Pacific, and Indian Oceans and under the polar ice cap. By staying near the maximum range, the SSBNs still threaten the major industrial and population centers of the Eastern Hemisphere, from Europe to the Far East, while making Soviet antisubmarine warfare more difficult.

The ninth and tenth Trident submarines, the *Tennessee* and the *West Virginia,* carry Trident II (D-5) missiles. Older Tridents will be modified to the D-5s. The older Poseidon SSBNs have been phased out within the last decade. Now at the turn of the new century, the SSBN force is composed entirely of quieter, more capable Trident SSBNs armed with D-5 missiles. This program has a price tag in excess of twenty billion dollars.

SSBNs have a single mission: to threaten the enemy's homeland with their ballistic missiles. Attack submarines are much more flexible and have a variety of missions. They are armed with torpedoes and/or cruise missiles, and can attack enemy submarines, surface ships, and land targets. They escort SSBNs going out or coming in from patrol. They patrol the choke points through which enemy submarines must pass. They keep sea-lanes clear for task groups or convoys. They pursue hostile SSBNs and other targets. And they conduct general searches of the ocean.

A fast-attack submarine often will operate at very low speeds, using only its passive sonar until enemy contact is made. Active sonar would be used briefly, perhaps only a single pulse, to confirm the target's range and bearing. Even that would be enough to alert the target, but would not give away the attack submarine's position. Should the search area prove free of the enemy, the attack submarine will proceed to another search area at top speed to minimize the time period in which it is at risk of being detected.

Submarines are ideal for clandestine operations because they can approach hostile shores unseen. They deliver mines, miniature submarines or submersibles, or small landing parties with equal ease. In World War II, submarines were used to deliver supplies to guerrillas, and to land and pick up raiding parties.

The *Nautilus* and the converted mine layer *Argonaut* delivered more than 200 U.S. Marines to Makin Island in the Gilberts in 1942, where they destroyed a seaplane base. The next year the *Nautilus* and the *Narwhal* delivered a raiding party to Attu in the Aleutians. The British also used submarines for clandestine operations on the coast of Nazi-occupied Europe.

The Axis also made imaginative use of their submarines. The Italian Navy used them to take miniature submarines and frogmen to enemy bases. Italian miniature submarines in World War II sank or severely damaged 63,000 tons of Allied warships and 50,000 tons of merchant shipping. A German submarine landed trained saboteurs on the eastern tip of Long Island in a famous incident of the war.

Diesel-powered submarines are particularly well suited for clandestine operations because they run more quietly underwater than do nuclear submarines. A Soviet Whiskey-class diesel submarine, apparently on a clandestine mission, ran aground in 1981 off the Swedish naval base at Karlskrona.

The Soviet Navy had special units called Spetsnaz to carry out clandestine operations off submarines. A Spetsnaz unit used a miniature submarine to reconnoiter Swedish naval bases in the Stockholm archipelago in October 1982. With an uncharacteristic bit of humor, a photograph of one of the Soviet miniature submarines was published in *Pravda* in the mid-1970s with the explanation that such vessels would be used to search for the lost city of Atlantis.

Less amusing is the possibility that miniature submarines might be used to lay nuclear mines at the exit points from U.S. and NATO submarine bases, or to interfere with such NATO seabed installations as the SOSUS sonar network.

The U.S. Navy has had two special forces: Underwater Demolition Teams (UDTs) and today's Sea-Air-Land (SEAL) teams. In World War II, UDTs cleared landing areas of mines and other obstructions, performed beach reconnaissance missions, and destroyed specific targets such as roads and bridges.

SEAL teams are made up of commandos who have been combat-trained to operate in hostile territory. A SEAL team is made up of twenty-seven officers and 156 enlisted men comprising five platoons, each capable of independent operations: reconnaissance, demolition, and sabotage. A SEAL team might be used, for example, to destroy an enemy SSBN base.

Several U.S. submarines have been converted to carry SEAL teams. The attack submarine *Grayback* was converted in 1967 to carry seven officers and sixty men and their specialized equipment. The *Grayback* operated out of the Subic Bay naval base in the Philippines. Two Ethan Allen–class nuclear-powered SSBNs, the *Sam Houston* and the *John Marshall*, later were converted to SEAL team carriers, greatly extending the range of possible clandestine operations.

Most antisubmarine engagements involve five stages: search, contact, approach, close combat, and disengagement. Sometimes the search is general, part of the protective measures for a convoy, say, or is dictated by information gained from SOSUS or satellites.

The search stage is carried out by what the Navy calls the "hunting platform"—surface warship, submarine, or aircraft—following a general search pattern, or as part of a task force patrolling a designated area. Like the submarine it seeks, the hunting platform wants to avoid detection and usually will employ passive sonar.

Detection and classification are both part of the contact stage. Once a possible target is discovered in the search area, the platform determines its speed and bearing, then whether it is really a submarine and not a merchant ship or a school of fish. The contact's acoustic signature is fed into the platform's computer. State-of-the-art equipment can determine from the acoustic signature the type, class, and sometimes even the individual submarine.

Now the platform begins the approach stage, tracking the target with passive sonar as it maneuvers into position to attack.

To attack, the hunter must be in a position to launch its weapons with reasonable certainty that they will hit the target. The weapon that is most risky is the torpedo, even though most modern torpedoes are equipped with sensors and wire-guidance links back to the launcher. Submarines attempt to compensate for torpedo unreliability by firing at targets at only half the torpedo's effective range of ten to twelve nautical miles.

If the first attack fails, the hunter and its target enter into close combat, each trying to destroy the other. Close combat between two submarines is the underwater equivalent of an aerial dogfight, and the performance capabilities of the individual submarine often is the determining factor.

After the battle comes disengagement, and usually a resumption of the search stage.

Denying the enemy the effective use of its submarines is the purpose of antisubmarine warfare, and this often can be accomplished without destroying them. This phase of naval warfare, the neutralization of enemy submarines, has the highest priority and commands a major portion of the naval budget.

The fast-attack submarine operates deep enough to take advantage of the ambient conditions of the ocean to avoid detection. It can spend long periods at sea. Its detection systems are capable of locating targets at considerable distances; its weapons can destroy targets with minimum risk to itself.

All this has made the attack submarine a difficult target for enemy surface ships. As a result, the most effective weapon against an attack submarine is another attack submarine. Yet surface task forces must be able to mount their own antisubmarine warfare operations.

Surface antisubmarine warfare involves two basic situations, the defense of naval vessels and the protection of merchantmen. Military experts assume that in a future war the areas of naval conflict are apt to be the major shipping lanes of the North Atlantic, and the Norwegian Sea, the Baltic, and the Mediterranean. On the other side of the world, the probable areas are the north and central Pacific.

To protect a large task force, three antisubmarine zones are formed. In the inner protection zone, warships and helicopters use active sonar to make sure the area is free of enemy submarines. Within this area, normally about sixty square miles, ships maneuver constantly to make it difficult for an attacking submarine to set up its weapons. The ships use hull-mounted sonar and may tow noisemakers to decoy a possible acoustic torpedo attack.

The middle zone is patrolled by ships and aircraft employing passive sonar. Ships use towed arrays, and helicopters use sonobuoys, allowing them to patrol a larger area than by dunking sonars.

The outer zone is in advance of the task force. Here long-range marine patrol (LRMP) aircraft such as the P-3 Orion and the S-3 Viking bring to bear the full panoply of detection systems, including radar, directional and nondirectional sonobuoys, and magnetic anomaly detector (MAD) equipment. Data from these systems is fed into the on-board computer. The aircraft are armed with torpedoes, missiles, and depth charges to attack any enemy submarine they locate.

On the edges of the outer zone are the fast-attack submarines, the hunter-killers, using their speed to cover large areas. These submarines operate on the assumption that anything they encounter is the enemy.

The constant zigzagging of its ships forces the task force to move slowly, probably not more than ten knots. The task force commander is in constant communication with the antisubmarine forces. He also receives information from satellite surveillance.

Should an enemy submarine be detected, it can be attacked by a variety of weapons, depending on how far the submarine is from the task force. A submarine more than five miles away would be attacked by helicopters using homing torpedoes and by frigates and destroyers released from their sectors to form an independent attack unit. These ships also would launch their own helicopters armed with torpedoes.

But positive sonar contact with a submarine is exceedingly difficult to establish. Ships often will search in vain for hours; the initial detection may have been in error, or the submarine realized it had been detected and fled.

One of the responsibilities of the force commander is to respond to a detected submarine. He can change course to move away from the danger area, but to do this every time may critically delay his mission. To frame the appropriate response, he establishes theoretical danger zones around the task force; the degree of danger inherent in each zone dictates the antisubmarine response.

The criteria for assessing potential threats involve what are called the limiting lines of submerged approach. They take into consideration the location of the submarine in relation to the task force, the speeds of each, and if and when the submarine can get in position to attack. In World War II these lines were entered by hand as overlays on plotting tables; today they are generated by computer and flashed on the commander's attack information screen. This data doesn't relieve the commander from making a judgment call, but it does help him weigh the risks.

The defense of merchant shipping is vital in the event of war. More then 99 percent of world trade still is carried by ship. Some thirty million tons of crude oil are delivered every day to Western Europe and America, most of it from the Middle East. Military experts estimate that in a major conflict 1,500 shiploads of oil per month would have to arrive in Western Europe to meet military and civilian needs.

This would mean a return to the large convoys of World War II, because large convoys afford better control and coordination and an efficient use of defensive resources. The use of convoys also forces submarines to come to the protected convoys and fight on terms of the convoy commander's choosing. A lesson from World War II: dispersing a convoy over a larger area means fewer ships sunk by submarines. At first ships were positioned at half-mile intervals; increasing the intervals to one mile cut losses by 25 percent.

Modern antisubmarine warfare equipment and techniques permit even greater spacing today. A convoy of forty ships spaced at two-mile intervals would cover an area of 750 square miles. This also would make the convoy much less vulnerable to attack by tactical nuclear weapons.

A convoy can be protected by its own escort or else by sailing through an area tactically dominated by other friendly forces. The second method is a more efficient use of naval forces.

A convoy support group would include ships with towed arrays, helicopters, LRMP aircraft, and one or more SSBN submarines. Such a group would use passive sonar in an area ahead of the convoy unhampered by the underwater noise of the convoy. The convoy would proceed on a zigzag course, confusing enemy submarines and making it harder for them to get into attack positions.

A submarine commander must know what is happening on the surface before he can attack, and many obstacles stand in his way. The information from satellite or air reconnaissance will be out of date by the time it is passed on to him. If he runs at top speed to intercept the convoy, his chances of being detected rise sharply. Once there, his sonar may be confused, either by the sheer underwater noise of the convoy or by acoustic deception equipment. If he goes near the surface to use his radar or periscope, he almost certainly will be detected.

Submarines armed with cruise missiles do not need to approach a convoy as closely as those armed only with torpedoes. The Russian Echo submarines carry the SS-N-3 Shaddock missiles with an estimated range of up to 300 nautical miles, but they have to surface to fire them. The Russian Charlie-class submarines can launch their SS-N-9 Siren missiles underwater, but they have an estimated top range of only one hundred miles.

In the event of a missile attack, electronic countermeasures cut down the chances of direct hits. Whether the threat is from submarines armed with torpedoes or missiles, the defensive strategy remains the same: confuse the submarine commander, force him to show himself, then destroy him. Once detected, a submarine should be destroyed before it can attack.

The most efficient way to turn a vague long-distance submarine contact into a target is by the use of aircraft. And submarines rarely are able to detect incoming aircraft until it is too late. The maritime patrol aircraft (MPA) is a workhorse of antisubmarine warfare with a special package of weapons, sensors, and target analysis equipment. The U.S. Navy's Lockheed S-3A Viking is carrier based, but most current MPAs are land based.

These planes carry magnetic anomaly detection (MAD) equipment, which is used to give a positive confirmation of an enemy submarine detection. The new Russian submarines with titanium hulls are impervious to MAD. The plane's radars and infrared devices can pick up a submarine's exposed periscope at great distances. Radar profiles can be displayed, giving instantaneous identification of the target. A bathythermograph buoy often is dropped to check on the salinity of the ocean, information that can be programmed into sonobuoys to make them more accurate. Sonobuoys can be set to operate at different depths in active or passive modes, directional or omnidirectional.

Aboard the plane a computerized central tactical system correlates data from the sensors, proposes weapon systems, and conducts the release of weapons. MPAs carry various types of torpedoes and depth bombs, armed with either nuclear or conventional warheads.

MPAs can operate independently or in support of a convoy, where they will be deployed as part of the defensive screen. They often operate in conjunction with antisubmarine warfare (ASW) helicopters from ships protecting the convoy. When assigned to area search tasks, MPAs operate independently, usually under a shore-based command.

Helicopters play an important role in protecting convoys because they can operate off small surface ships. Initially helicopters were considered extensions of the ship's sensor and weapon delivery systems, but they have evolved into fully autonomous antisubmarine hunter-killers armed with homing torpedoes and depth bombs.

The ASW helicopter carries a dunking sonar, a unique surveillance device that often is more effective than a sonobuoy because it can be lowered through the sonar-deflecting thermocline to home in on otherwise undetectable targets. The passive mode is used on dunking sonar if it is believed that the submarine doesn't suspect it has been detected; the active mode when the submarine is moving into an attack position. Helicopters usually work in pairs, one working the dunking sonar, the other ready to attack.

To sense the grand strategy of submarine and antisubmarine warfare, it is instructive to look at the Greenland–Iceland–United Kingdom (GIUK) gap. Military experts believe that in an East-West conflict ships and submarines of the Russian Northern Fleet would attempt to break out of northern waters into the Atlantic through the GIUK gap, while other Russian ships and submarines would try to reach the North Sea through the Skagerrak, the waters separating Norway and Sweden from Denmark.

NATO considers both the GIUK gap and the Skagerrak choke points and has taken measures to seal them up. This involves fixed monitoring devices like seabed sonar, augmented by patrolling submarines, and ASW aircraft. Should a war seem imminent, U.S. and NATO forces would undoubtedly enter the area. (This scenario is the basis of Tom Clancy's novel *Red Storm Rising,* which imagines a non-nuclear East-West war.)

11 | The Cold War's End Brings New Problems

The armament agreements that followed the end of the Cold War brought sharp reductions to both the American and Russian submarine fleets. Currently the Russians have 70 submarines to America's 73, but the gap becomes much greater when one looks at the rest of the two navies. The Russians have 1 aircraft carrier, the U.S. has 12; the Russians have 7 cruisers, the U.S. has 27; and the Russians have 17 destroyers, the U.S. 55. The Russian Navy has 171,500 active personnel, the U.S. 367,679.

During the 1990s, most of the Russian defense budget went to the army and the air force to support the war in Chechnya. As a result, Russian submarines aren't being properly maintained. On April 7, 1989, the *Komsomolets* sank off the Norwegian coast after a fire broke out aboard, and 42 of the 69 crew members perished.

In 1999, a routine check of the submarine *Pantera* turned up something terribly wrong. Someone had stolen valuable palladium metal from the vessel's oxygen regeneration systems, which purify the air while the sub is submerged. Useless coal dust had been put in its place. An investigation revealed that the culprit was an officer on the submarine, who risked his own and his shipmates' lives for $9,000.

Russia's once proud Northern Fleet is so starved for funds that admirals can't maintain their shrinking armada. Ships come to port for overhaul, never to sail again. Equipment—including cranes used to load nuclear missiles—is beginning to fall apart. Sailors from the submarine *Voronezh* were able to get a dilapidated dormitory remodeled only because its namesake city raised the funds.

The Russian navy has other problems. Some 120 decommissioned submarines are rusting off the Russian coastline near Murmansk. They are time bombs. If they sink, nuclear waste will ruin the environment, and there is also the danger that they might explode.

It seemed as if a disaster was inevitable. When it came, ironically, it struck one of the Russian navy's newest and most powerful cruise-missile submarines, the *Kursk*. The Russian navy was in the Barents Sea for the most extensive naval maneuvers in several years. Thirty vessels were involved, and it was to be an occasion of pride and triumph. On the second day, August 13, 2000, Captain Gennadi Lyachin was preparing to put his submarine through its paces with the task force. Five high-ranking Northern Fleet staff officers were aboard the *Kursk* to observe the exercise.

By midday, the *Kursk* had completed a torpedo-firing run and was preparing for another. Captain Lyachin, 45, one of the Russian navy's most experienced submarine officers, radioed the task-force commander for permission to fire. The transmission was monitored by the American surveillance ship U.S.N.S. *Loyal,* lurking about 186 miles west-northwest of the *Kursk,* as was the commander's "permission granted." But instead of the sounds of torpedoes being blown from launch tubes, sonar operators aboard U.S. submarines working with the *Loyal,* heard two explosions, one short and sharp, the second an enormous, thundering boom. A Norwegian seismic institute also recorded the explosions and said the second carried the force of two tons of TNT, registering 3.5 on the Richter scale.

Later, evidence obtained from underwater cameras showed that the blast tore open the entire double-hulled forward section of the 505-ft. vessel, an area the size of a school gymnasium. Seawater would have slammed into the torpedo and cruise-missile compartments, instantly killing the men on duty there. In the control room just aft of the shattered weapons compartments, Lyachin, the five officers and the dozen or so petty officers manning the ship's controls would have had no time to react before the combined power of the blast and sea water tore through, destroying the arrays of switches, computers and video screens that constitute the "brain" of a submarine. All would have been killed outright or quickly drowned. From there the water was likely to have cascaded through passageways and doors and into the "sail," the conning tower above the control room and into communications spaces and living quarters just aft of the sail. At that point, the floodwaters were probably thwarted by thick, watertight bulkheads guarding the twin VM-5 pressurized water reactors powering the submarine.

However, there would be no hope for the men whose duties placed them in the reactor control rooms and the turbine and machinery spaces behind the reactor. The flash flooding in the forward part of the *Kursk* would have caused the bow to drop, pitching the 14,000-ton submarine into a steep dive with steam turbines still delivering power to its twin screws. In seconds, the sub would have pounded into the seabed some 350 ft. beneath the storm-driven surface of the Barents with a shock that would have hurled survivors against equipment and bulkheads.

Finally, as the submarine settled onto the ocean floor, openings along the keel would probably no longer have been able to draw in the seawater needed to cool the reactors. Automatic systems would have "scrammed" the reactors, pushing control rods into the core and shutting them down. The *Kursk,* its shattered bow shoved into a furrow of sand and heeling to port, lay silent, without power or head or light or hope, its 118 souls dead or doomed.

"The majority of the crew was in the part of the boat that was hit by the catastrophe that developed at lightning speed," said Ilya Klebanov, Deputy Prime Minister and head of a commission investigating the sinking. It was all over, he said, "in the space of two minutes, more or less." The tapping out of SOS signals in Morse code indicated that some crew members survived for a time in the stern sections of the boat, but Adal Vyacheslav Popov, commander of the Northern Fleet, admitted that no tapping had been heard from the submarine since two days after the accident.

The sailors who did survive the initial flooding would have come to envy the dead. Dying always seems more gruesome when it is in slow motion. And slow-motion submarine deaths are particularly and perversely compelling when they happen in shallow water within reach of rescuers. Men who have been trapped in stricken submarines say the crew of the *Kursk* would have suffered from cold as temperature fell to 41 degrees Fahrenheit and from severe headaches as levels of carbon dioxide rose in the smothering atmosphere. They also would have suffered from fear and hopelessness as rescuers repeatedly tried, and failed, to save them. "Those guys can hear the mini-subs," explained a U.S. Navy officer. "Listening to that for any length of time as you're slowly suffocating would drive anyone nuts."

By the end of the week, any men still alive would have been sliding toward death. As the CO_2 level rose, their brains would have slowly turned off, as if on a dimmer switch; consciousness would have ebbed to coma, and reality would have faded to black.

What caused the loss of the *Kursk* remains unexplained. In the first days of the disaster, Russian officials fell back on old Soviet habits of secrecy and confusion. They made no announcements for two days, then issued a bland statement that there had been a "technical fault" and that the boat was on the sea bottom. After the seriousness of the accident became clearer, Defense Minister Igor Sergeyev declared that there was "incontrovertible evidence" that the submarine had collided with another vessel. In past years Soviet and U.S. vessels have had near collisions while spying on each other, but the Pentagon firmly rejected any suggestion that any U.S. submarines were involved.

Later, Russian officials dropped the collision claim and blamed an explosion in the weapons area, a theory supported by Western experts, who said it could have come from a torpedo or missile or a high-pressure air tank used to blow ballast water when surfacing. The *Kursk,* according to *Jane's Fighting Ships,* normally carries 24 cruise missiles able to deliver either 1,650 lbs. of high explosives or a nuclear warhead a distance of 300 miles, plus as many as 28 torpedoes with similar warhead capability. The Russians said the *Kursk* was carrying no nuclear weapons under an agreement with the U.S. that neither side would deploy tactical nuclear weapons.

Klebanov clung to the collision theory, saying that the submarine hit a "huge, heavy object" of "very large tonnage" that tore open the boat's hull, but offered no suggestions about what that object might have been, and there were no reports of a surface ship in the area with severe hull damage.

Whatever the direct cause of the disaster, the *Kursk* was doomed as much by under-funding, insufficient training, and incompetent military management as by collision or high explosives. Since the end of the Cold War, the Russian navy has declined from 613 ships of all types to around 95 today, a drop of 84 percent, compared with shrinkage of around 40 percent for Western navies. Of the few ships remaining in the Russian inventory, only about 10 percent are considered by Western experts to be fit to put to sea. There is little money for maintenance, and the result can be seen in naval bases all around Russia, where ships lie in rusting rows, crewed by unmotivated and often unpaid sailors.

"Because of poor maintenance levels across much of the fleet, the fleet can't put to sea very often, so personnel are less well trained," says Joanna Kidd, naval analyst at the London-based International Institute for Strategic Studies. The *Kursk*, as one of the newest and most important submarines in the fleet, would have received enough to keep up maintenance but probably not enough to keep up vital sea-time training for its crew. "It's speculation, but their reactions might have been slow," Kidd said. Similarly, the rescue efforts may have suffered from lack of training. "If most of the Russian navy can hardly put to sea, then it's doubtful whether they have practiced this type of [rescue] operation very often."

The exercise in which the *Kursk* was lost reflected President Vladimir Putin's declared intention to rebuild the navy at least to the levels of the French and British fleets, if not to the size of the mighty U.S. Navy. The maneuvers in the Barents Sea were intended to be a dress rehearsal for a show-of-force cruise of the eastern Mediterranean later this year to be led by the aircraft carrier *Admiral Kuznetsov* and the battle cruiser *Peter the Great*. Losing the *Kursk* is a major setback for these plans and for President Putin's naval ambitions. "He has aligned himself personally with the revival of the navy's fortune's," said Kidd. "This is a big humiliation for him."

Perhaps this is why Putin had so little to say as the *Kursk* disaster unfolded. He left for his summer-vacation retreat in Sochi on the day of the accident and sent no messages of condolence to the fleet or to the furious families of the missing men. His officially published schedule told of phone conversations with foreign leaders but made no mention of briefings, consultations or expressions of concern about the *Kursk*. Five days after the disaster, a casually dressed Putin met with visiting academics to discuss at length problems of science, research and the brain drain. After the meeting, in response to journalists' questions, he reluctantly acknowledged that the situation with the *Kursk* was "critical" and said, "All necessary and possible efforts to save the crew have been carried out."

But had they? For crucial days, Russian officials had rejected Western offers of help, including the dispatch of U.S., French, British, and Norwegian rescue equipment to the scene of the disaster. On the third day Putin ordered Admiral Vladimir Kuroyedov, the navy Commander in Chief, to accept help. The Russians promptly invited Norway and Britain to send equipment, but by then it was already a near certainty that any survivors would perish before the rescuers could reach the area. In fact, shortly before the British team arrived, the Northern Fleet commander said, "The critical line of survivability has been closed."

Russian officials have talked of attaching floats to the hull, inflating them and lifting what is left of the *Kursk* to the surface. But with much of the hull flooded, the 14,000-ton submarine could now be a water-logged 30,000 tons, even more difficult to handle. A chilling alternative is to leave it on the seabed, along with the six other nuclear submarines, four of them Russian, that have sunk in the age of the atom. The double steel hull of the *Kursk* will provide some containment for the reactors, which are encased in heavy, steel pressure vessels. The submarine would provide a grim and poignant memorial to the 118 sailors who served, and died, onboard.

The loss of the submarine *Thresher* with 129 sailors aboard in 1963 prompted the U.S. Navy to launch the SUBSAFE program. It's designed to wring as much danger as possible out of the inherently risky business of prowling beneath the surface of the world's oceans. The program isn't perfect. In 1968, the U.S.S. *Scorpion* went down, killing all 99 aboard. But those 288 Americans lost are fewer than half the number of Russians lost serving in the Russian nuclear-submarine force, counting those who perished on the *Kursk.*

A U.S. submarine hasn't been lost for more than 30 years, as a result of a rigorous certification program that gives each key piece of a submarine—including its hull, pipes, valves and flood barriers—a serial number pinpointing its source and whom to hold accountable if it fails. Critical systems are duplicated. For example, there are three ways to empty the ballast on Trident submarines. Crews are repeatedly drilled, ashore and afloat, with two key aims: to keep their sub safe and, if that fails, to get out alive. The top concerns for crews include knowing how to restrict flooding once the hull has been breached and how to put out a fire.

Submariners say they drill more often and more realistically than their Russian counterparts. While the Russians have automated much of their onboard machinery, the U.S. still relies heavily on men in the loop standing watch to keep their vessel humming and safe.

Trouble can crop up unexpectedly on a submarine. In March, 2000 a warning flare exploded in its launch tube in a submerged submarine. The blast sheared a dozen bolts holding the launcher in place and let seawater flow into the bow compartment. There were no injuries, and the Navy has now barred the use of that kind of flare.

If all this engineering and training fails, the Navy maintains a rescue sub perpetually on alert in San Diego. Built in the wake of the *Thresher*'s loss, it is designed to reach trapped submariners anywhere in the world within three days. It could have come—had the Russians asked—to the aid of the *Kursk.*

Bibliography

Barron, John. *Breaking the Ring: The Bizarre Case of the Walker Family Spy Ring.* Boston: Houghton Mifflin Company, 1987.

Beach, Capt. Edward L. (Ret.) *The United States Navy: 200 Years.* New York: Henry Holt and Company, 1986.

Beebe, William. *Half Mile Down.* New York: Duell, Sloan & Pearce, Inc., 1934.

Burgess, Robert F. *Ships Beneath the Sea: A History of Subs and Submersibles.* New York: McGraw-Hill Book Company, 1975.

Campbell, Christy. *Weapons of War: Present and Future Weapons, Systems and Strategies.* New York: Peter Bedrick Books, 1983.

Carlucci, Frank C. *Annual Report to the Congress, Fiscal Year 1989.* Washington, D.C.: Department of Defense, U.S. Government Printing Office, 1988.

————. *Soviet Military Power: An Assessment of the Threat.* Washington, D.C.: Department of Defense, U.S. Government Printing Office, 1988.

Carter, Jimmy. *Why Not the Best?* New York: Bantam, 1976.

Chief of Naval Operations, Office of. *Understanding Soviet Naval Developments.* Washington, D.C.: Department of the Navy, U.S. Government Printing Office, 1985.

Piccard, Jacques. *The Sun Beneath the Sea.* New York: Charles Scribner's Sons, 1971.

Polmar, Norman, and Thomas B Allen. *Rickover: Controversy and Genius.* New York: Simon and Schuster, 1982.

Preston, Anthony. *Submarines.* New York: St. Martin's Press, Inc., 1982.

Roscoe, Theodore. *Submarine Operations in World War II.* Boston: Little Brown, 1972.

Sulzberger, C. S. *The American Heritage History of World War II.* New York: Bonanza Books, 1966.

Sweeney, James B. *A Pictorial History of Oceanographic Submersibles.* New York: Crown Publishers, Inc., 1970.

Verne, Jules. *Twenty Thousand Leagues Under the Sea.* New York: The Heritage Press, 1956.

Wyckoff, James. *Who Really Invented the Submarine?* New York: G. P. Putnam's Sons, 1965.

Index

Photo Credits

The Bettmann Archive, New York: 34, 37, 38, 133, 139
Collection Imperial War Museum, London: 87, 94 (Copyright the Estate of John Hamilton)
The National Archive, Washington, DC: 78, 93, 103, 107, 99, 108
The Nautilus Memorial Submarine Force Library and Museum, Groton, CT: 36, 40, 43, 48, 52, 54,
    57, 58, 59, 63, 77, 82, 101, 102 (bottom), 119, 174
The Naval Historical Center, Washington, DC: 47
OAR/National Undersea Research Program (NURP): 145
US Navy Photos: 2, 3, 4, 6, 7, 9, 13, 16, 18, 19, 23, 24, 95, 109, 115, 126, 143, 156, 159, 161, 162, 164,
    176, 177
Wide World Photos, New York: 72, 87, 89, 97, 105, 118, 135